THE DEBT TRAP

How Did We Get In?
How Do We Get Out?

William V. Thompson
with Fatin H. Horton

Treasure House
An Imprint of
Destiny Image® Publishers, Inc.
P.O. Box 310
Shippensburg, PA 17257-0310

"For where your treasure is,
there will your heart be also." Matthew 6:21

ISBN 1-56043-335-3

For Worldwide Distribution
Printed in the U.S.A.

First Printing: 1999   Second Printing: 2000

This book and all other Destiny Image, Revival Press, Mercy Place, Fresh Bread, and Treasure House books are available at Christian bookstores and distributors worldwide.

For a U.S. bookstore nearest you, call **1-800-722-6774**.
For more information on foreign distributors, call **717-532-3040**.
Or reach us on the Internet: **http://www.reapernet.com**

Contents

Foreword

I have known the author for more than 14 years and have been personally blessed by the financial insight the Lord has given him. When I read the rough manuscript, I said to myself, "Here's another 'masterpiece of truth' that will be liberating to the Body of Christ at large."

I highly recommend this book to every pastor. They should consider having these principles taught in their churches as either a class or a weekend seminar.

It's been stated that there are two books that will change the world—the Bible and the checkbook. I believe that God has raised up this author for such a time as this to teach us how to overcome the "NSF Syndrome" and to balance the checkbook. May God bless this apostle of finance.

Pastor Otis Lockett, Sr.
Evangel Fellowship Church

Introduction

In 1997, more Americans filed bankruptcy (1.3 million) than graduated from college. This happened in a strong and healthy economy. What will happen when the economy takes a downward turn?

This book has one purpose, *to expose the true nature of debt.* We have been told by economists, the Federal Reserve Board, and accountants that debt is good for the nation; however, it is debt that is destroying the very core of our lives, our families, and our nation. *Debt is the visible manifestation of an invisible devil,* and just like the devil, its purpose is to steal, kill, and destroy (see Jn. 10:10).

Like any other disease, unless a cure is found for it, debt will continue its rampage and destruction throughout the nation and the world. Before a vaccine can be created to combat a disease or before an enemy can be destroyed, one must understand that disease's or enemy's structure, function, action, and purpose. To defeat debt, you must gain an insightful understanding of its total makeup. In this book, we totally expose debt so that you may declare war on it in your life and be successful in defeating it.

Without knowing the enemy, you're destined for destruction. The will of God is that in this season, you turn the tables on the enemy and totally annihilate debt in your life.

Chapter 1

The Debt Trap

Prior to the Emancipation Proclamation of 1865, there were 4 million slaves in America. Today, there are *over* 1.3 million known slaves in the United States. These are people who filed bankruptcy in 1997. It is projected that an additional 7.2 million people will file bankruptcy within the next five years.

As the number of these slaves continues to increase, so does the power of the debt trap. Everyone whom you owe is your master, from your bank and lending institution to your credit card company, and even to your friends. *If you are in debt, then you are a slave* (see Prov. 22:7). You have been caught by the debt trap and, except God be your help, you won't escape.

Debt is a perpetual cycle that feeds off of your hard work and poor stewardship. *People in debt can't produce a different outcome following the same process*, so whatever you did to get in debt must cease in order for you to get out.

Banks send letters to congratulate you on your approval for a loan. Would you congratulate someone who just found out that he or she had cancer, just received a jail sentence, or is in an abusive relationship? As absurd as that sounds, we celebrate debt. But in this book *we declare war on debt and expose it as an enemy to the will of God in our lives!*

The Setting

A story is told of a young girl and her friend on a beautiful spring day. Both were students at Florida State University and, with the weather so nice, they decided that it was an ideal day to skip class. After pondering their options, they chose to take a trip to Seminole Reservation, a local park with a lake.

When first arriving at the lake, it looked like a beach. Off to the sides, however, were an abundance of trees. Normally the friends would ride the paddleboats, but today they felt like trying something different. They spotted a rowboat and decided to row away from shore. They didn't need to do much rowing, for the current of the water was strong enough to propel the boat.

The experience was breathtaking. The sunlight glistened off the water, with its rays bouncing off the disturbance of the currents. Sunlight peeked through the covering of the trees, creating a broken shadow effect. The sound of the water being divided under them was a serene trickle, relaxing to the mind. This ride propelled them into another dimension, causing them to totally lose focus of their responsibilities as students, their distance from shore, and the fact that they didn't know how to row the boat.

After an hour of relaxing, the girls decided that they were ready to return to shore. It was then that they realized just how far they had gone out. Immediately they grabbed the oars and attempted to row back to shore. However, there was a technique to rowing the boat that they hadn't learned. Immediately panic set in. *They were in a situation they couldn't handle.* They had all the equipment that they needed to get back to shore, but because they didn't know how to use it, *they were stuck in their problem situation.*

How did they get out of their problem? There was a young man sailing in their area. They flagged him down and he extended a rope to them and pulled them to shore.

The Deception of Debt

This story is a perfect example of how the debt trap works. Debt's deception has people believing that they can handle situations they are unprepared for. The temptation of a beautiful day caused the girls to forsake their responsibilities as students. The day was too good to miss by attending class. Likewise, when debt makes an offer, it's packaged as an experience too good to pass up.

Notice the appearance of the situation. At first glance, the lake area looked like a beach, but after closer inspection, the girls noticed the presence of trees and woods. Debt creates distractions that cause you to focus on immediate gratification and prevent you from seeing the total picture and weighing all the factors.

Interest plays the role of the water current, because it multiplies the effect of your purchase on your finances. Just as the girls didn't have to do much rowing to get far out on the lake, it doesn't take much purchasing, with extremely high interest, to get you swamped in debt. The interest propels you to a point of helplessness. As your debt remains, interest accrues and the debt enlarges, taking you further and further out until you reach that point of helplessness.

When you first get out there, however, the experience is exhilarating. There is excitement from making a new purchase that takes your mind off bills, problems, responsibilities, and concerns, and gives you a sense of peace. It is at this moment that the dangers of the debt trap begin to take effect. Slow to respond to the danger of unpaid bills, you fail to realize that the situation has become more than you can handle. Suddenly, reality steps back into the picture and you realize that your present situation is out of control. ***The debt trap has caught you!***

The Proponents of the Debt Trap

So who sets up this trap and wants you in debt? The devil is the obvious answer, but the important thing is to discern who he's using. Think of the people and groups who profit from your debt. The **government** wants you in debt because borrowing stimulates the economy. Consumers' buying frenzies create jobs and increase the money supply. **Banks** profit from the interest earned. Your **employer** knows that as long as you are in debt and owe bills, you will be motivated to work. The company knows that you need this job to pay your debt, which gives it greater control over you. **People who are in debt** want you in debt because misery loves company. **Mortgage, finance,** and **credit card companies** all profit from your debt. They know that the more you buy, the more they make.

Consider that banks, once called your "savings institutions," now refer to themselves as your "lending institutions." Even **people in debt** are undecided about being debt-free. While their mouths say that they want to be free, their actions prove otherwise. They continue to use credit cards, seek new loans, and refuse to prepare and follow a budget. All these groups, as well-meaning and beneficial as their services may be, need your debt to stay in business. *God is the only one who wants you out of debt; therefore, He's willing to help you.* Money is a big part of our lives and the devil knows that if he can influence our money, he can have a greater influence in our lives.

How early can you get caught in the trap?

The devil sees the potential of your future and uses debt to try to abort it. The debt trap can catch you at any and all stages of life. Statistics show that two percent of 12- to 15-year-olds and seven percent of 16- and 17-year-olds have their own credit cards. Additionally, the majority of children are authorized users of their parents' credit cards. This perpetuates a habit of buying on credit without experiencing the responsibility of paying the debt.

Additionally, debt teaches our children that they can have something *now* without working to pay for it. *Credit purchasing allows them to fill up their present while emptying their future.* As children go into the real world, they take this habit with them and are hit head on with the responsibility of having to pay the balance when they are unprepared to handle it. They are prime candidates for the debt trap.

As adults, we often take the attitude that our possessions define our identity (see Lk. 12:15). Thousands of Christians get in debt every year competing with a standard set by the world (e.g., what's seen on television, in magazines, and in movies) without taking into account whether or not they can afford the items. Though they appear to be blessed, their financial condition proves otherwise.

It is the will of God that senior citizens be debt-free. However, many senior citizens take a "reverse mortgage," which is a loan that pays them monthly until their death. It serves as supplemental income, many times to pay for existing debts. When they die, they leave their family their debts and take from their children's inheritance (see Prov. 19:14; Neh. 5:1-5 TLB). Not only does the reverse mortgage have to be paid back, but so do the debts that were left unpaid at death. Debt has accomplices and it's important that the Body of Christ and people in general recognize them.

How do you feel in the debt trap?

Debt produces feelings of hopelessness, oppression, and mind control. In the story about the two girls on the lake, think of all the things that could have gone through those girls' minds and compare them to your thoughts about your debts. When they saw that there was nothing they could do, they probably thought about their rescue. Would they ever get out of the situation? Was there anyone nearby who could help them? Surely they weighed all their options. What are your options when you're in debt? Based on the Word of God, you are *permanently* obligated to your creditors until the bills are paid unless *they* (not God) release you from it (see Ps. 37:21; Lev. 25).

Notice that it took another person to help them get out of their situation. Just like those girls, unless you know how to handle the resources that you've been given, it will take someone else to help you get out of your present situation.

We took a survey of about 100 Christians and asked the question, "How does debt make you feel?" Some of their responses included the following:

Stressed out. People felt like their debt was a heavy load. They felt like it was pulling them in many different directions.

Embarrassed. People didn't understand how they, as Spirit-filled believers, could allow such a thing to happen. Debt had robbed them of their witness to their co-workers, creditors, and bankers.

Depressed. Debt releases a spirit of depression that is a catalyst for the feelings of hopelessness, inadequacy, and helplessness.

Confused. People said that their confusion caused them to forsake writing a plan to get out of debt, returning creditors' calls, and keeping focused on their entire financial situation. They were totally disoriented and ineffective.

Fearful. People were afraid that other bad things would happen because of their debt. *They literally felt cursed!* Some people were too afraid to even open their mail!

This is no psychological analysis. These are the results of asking born-again, Spirit-filled believers who are currently in debt how they feel on a *daily basis.* How many of these feelings do you share when you think about the money that you owe to creditors?

Slavery

Since we now understand how the debt trap works, what is its purpose? The obvious purpose of the debt trap is to get us so far in debt that we feel like we can't get out. *Debt can be described as the devil's twin,* based on First Peter 5:8. They are fraternal, not identical, meaning that they are birthed from the same womb but don't look alike. The devil is the product of unrighteousness and self-righteousness. Debt is produced in the same manner; it comes through either unrighteousness such as greed or covetousness (sin, see First John 5:17), or self-righteousness (pride, see Proverbs 16:18).

In First Peter 5:8, the devil is described as "your adversary" and someone "seeking whom he may devour." Debt works the same way. It is a direct enemy to the will of God for your life. Debt wants to rob you of your worship, your witness, your will, your wealth, and a number of other things that will be discussed in a later chapter. But the biggest thing that debt wants to rob you of is your *freedom*. This type of slavery has never been a racial issue, but an economical one.

Solomon said that "the borrower is servant [slave] to the lender" (Prov. 22:7b), showing us how debt makes you a slave. Debt masters you by literally controlling your life. It tells you where to live and when to work. You can't miss a day of work due to sickness because of the bills that need to be paid that month. Every aspect of your finances and life must bow to its power. *Nothing* can be done without first considering the debt that you owe, including the paying of your tithe and offering. When in total control, debt has the power to make you serve another god. When this happens, you know that the debt trap has caught you.

To illustrate how this slavery is a modern-day phenomenon, let's say that you pay $4,000 in interest over a year's time. Your salary is $10 per hour (approximately $21,000 per year). By dividing the $4,000 interest by your hourly salary of $10, you will find that you would have been enslaved ***400 hours*** or ***50 work days***. That's almost 2½ out of 12 months that you were a slave to debt and interest.

The debt trap's design

The debt trap can be compared to a bear trap. Bear traps are usually well concealed, but when they snap, they are literally impossible to get out of. The debt trap is hidden in unaffordable pleasures, incorrect teaching on money, and religious overtones that make excuses for a Christian's poor stewardship (e.g., "God develops you by allowing you to incur debt"). It is also found in family and friends who have a need but who are not qualified to receive our help, whether it be through not paying their tithe and offering (see Mal. 3:8-10) or by being lazy and refusing to work (see 2 Thess. 3:9-10).

Bankruptcy

People caught in the debt trap begin to think about possible solutions to their problem, much like the girls in the rowboat at the beginning of the chapter. Over one million people chose bankruptcy as an option in 1997. As a Christian, is bankruptcy a viable option for your situation? According to the Word of God, *no*! Consider Psalm 37:21, which says, "The wicked borroweth, and payeth not again: but the righteous showeth mercy, and giveth." The courts may release you from your debts, but God doesn't. A vow that must be paid was made in taking the vendor's product or service (see Eccles. 5:4).

Also, consider the spiritual impact. *If you file bankruptcy and are a member of a church, the courts have the legal right to require your church to refund up to 12 months of your tithe and offerings.* Now the debt trap has snared innocent people. In addition, your creditors have not received their money, resulting in loss of income to their families. Their employees may not get paid or even have a job, which results in their inability to pay their bills—all because you refused to take personal responsibility for *your* bills. That's five groups of people—you and your family, the Body of Christ, your creditors' families, your creditors' employees and their families, and their creditors—who must suffer because of your lack of discipline.

If a Christian files bankruptcy, he must first prove (based on the Word of God) that he has made every attempt in his power to pay his creditors back *and* has a plan to pay back what he owes his creditors, regardless of whether the courts hold him responsible or not. The releasing of all debts was a part of the Year of Jubilee (see Lev. 25), but it was only amongst the Israelites; heathen nations were not involved. Most of the time bankruptcy is a result of poor stewardship and bad decisions. You are the only one who should suffer for your decisions. If you *must file bankruptcy*, we believe that there is a certain process you must go through to salvage character and integrity.

1. Sell your assets to try to pay your creditors (see 2 Kings 4:7; Mt. 18:25).
2. Contact your creditors, informing them of your intention to file bankruptcy and get their release (see Mt. 18:26-27).
3. Consult wise Christians for financial counseling (see Prov. 12:14; 20:18 TLB)
4. Tap your 401K, home equity, or any reasonable source (see 2 Kings 4:7; Mt. 18:25).
5. Develop a plan to pay back your creditors what you owe them. Even though the courts release you, God doesn't! (See Psalm 37:21.)

There must be a difference between the holy and unholy!

Get Your Vision Back

Close your eyes and imagine what life would be like *totally debt-free*. This is what God sees. There are no bills, with the exception of your necessary living expenses. You own your home, your car, and all accessories that come with your house. You are *totally debt-free*. How do you feel? Do you like what you're feeling? ***If so, never forget the feeling.*** (Do this daily.)

Now, go and write down what you saw. The Bible tells us to write down the vision, so that whoever reads it may run with it (see Hab. 2:2). Those were specific instructions that the Lord gave to the prophet concerning his question and were the solution to his problem. Writing down what you see is key to your becoming totally debt-free! ***If you see what others don't see, you'll have what others don't have.***

Though you may be caught in the debt trap and enslaved by debt, see yourself free, for there is an appointed time for your deliverance. Our experience in counseling others shows that people can be debt-free (except their mortgage) in approximately two years. If you'll work two years of your life like others won't, you'll spend the rest of your life like others can't.

The key to success is knowing that *you can't produce a different outcome following the same process.* When you change your habits, you will change your destiny. In the following chapters, we will perform a detailed analysis on debt so that you can understand it to overtake it.

Debt has set a trap to ultimately destroy the purpose of God in your life. We believe that the biggest thing that hinders the people of God from completing their divine assignments and reaching their divine destiny is not the devil, but debt. Whenever we can break free from the trap that debt has set in our life, then we can defeat it.

Chapter 2

The Person: Who Is Debt?

Debt has caught you in a trap of overspending and poor stewardship. Before you can defeat debt, you must know who debt is. The purpose of this chapter is to shed light on debt's identity. We have established debt as a direct enemy to the will of God for our lives, but how does this enemy manifest itself?

A Contagious Disease

Webster's Dictionary defines a disease as "an unhealthy condition." Debt has an effect that potentially touches every aspect of life. We see debt as a contagious disease that contaminates the entire family. In Second Kings 4:1-7, we find a woman whose husband had just died, and the creditors were coming to take her two sons as payment for her husband's debt.

In biblical days, repayment of past due debts was a process (see Neh. 5:1-5). First, creditors would take your cloak. Next you would be forced to mortgage any vineyards and lands. If there was still outstanding debt, you were forced to mortgage your home. If debts were still unpaid, creditors came and took your children to be bondsmen.

In biblical Hebrew, the word for bondsman means "slave." We see that this man of God (the Bible says that he was of the sons of the prophets) had created a precarious situation for his entire family by his debt. When looking at debt as a disease, close relationship allowed the disease to spread throughout his entire family, costing them all their possessions, and nearly leading to their sons' enslavement for life. Though he was a prophet, he was still a slave. Debt has not changed. Even today, parents are getting into astronomical debt by buying things on credit and so set their children up for future slavery.

The cancerous spreading (Neh. 5:1-5)

The disease of debt has deadly side effects that deteriorate the spiritual equivalents to the five senses. Debt releases a sense of hopelessness and frustration. The Bible says that the woman cried (see 2 Kings 4:1), which lets us know that she was probably at wits' end and knew of nothing else to do. This frustration leads to the assumptions that debt is a part of life and that nothing can be done to change it.

This loss of faith is a sign of a loss of being able to **hear** the voice of God. Romans 10:17 tells us that faith is produced by hearing the spoken word of God. Therefore, if we are losing faith, it's because debt is taking away our ability to hear.

It is at this point of faithlessness that debt begins to kill any **vision** (sight) that you have of living a debt-free life (see Prov. 29:18). There are people reading this book who can't see themselves as being debt-free. If you can't see it, it won't happen.

Next, debt begins to destroy your sense of **smell**. In Genesis 27:27, Isaac smelled the clothes of Jacob and said that Jacob's smell was as a field that the Lord had blessed. There is an ability to literally "sniff out" the blessings of the Lord; however, when we're in debt, we tend to lose that ability.

Studies show that 50 percent of **taste** is smell. Therefore, if we can't smell, it reduces our ability to "taste and see that the Lord is good" (Ps. 34:8a). All that is left is your sense of touch. However, worrying about bills hinders us from **feeling** the presence of God. When the process is complete, debt has turned you into a spiritual vegetable, totally subject to its enslaving power.

Effects and ramifications

As the disease begins to spread, it manifests itself in physical symptoms. Many people trapped in the web of debt have low self-esteem and feel guilt and shame. They rationalize, *If I can make these mistakes with my finances, I will probably make similar mistakes in my ministry, marriage, or other important area of my life.*

This gives the mind-set that debt is insurmountable. It becomes harder to worship or even think clearly because your mind is so consumed with worrying about debt. Debt and bills cause people to become irritable. Think of how many arguments you and your spouse have had over the abundance of debt and bills you have.

Financial problems are one of the leading causes of divorce in this country. Parents are always working to pay off debts; therefore, they have no time for their spouse or children. The children grow up with a misconception of what family life should be, couples don't have time to enrich their marriage, and personal health and ministry are all neglected because of debt.

Many times people feel stressed by debt, which causes sickness in their body. That, in turn, forces them to stay home, and thus takes away their ability to work.

Point of contact

The woman in Second Kings 4 was lamenting over the debt *that her husband had incurred.* He died, leaving her and her children an inheritance of debts, simply based on relationship. We assume that it was the husband who was responsible for the debt due to his position as head of the household. The wife had done nothing to contribute to the accumulation of debt, yet she now was totally responsible for it. Even today, children and spouses are inheriting the debts of deceased family members, despite the fact that they played no role in acquiring that debt.

There is a disease that is said to have originated in Africa about five years ago, called the Ebola virus. This disease is so deadly that if an infected person even breathes on you, you become infected. The disease has five levels of severity, with the deadliest being named Ebola Sudan. It liquefies your internal organs and causes you to implode and literally regurgitate them. Blood then flows out of every opening in your body until your death.

Debt is a financial version of the Ebola virus. It is highly contagious, sometimes just by contact. People co-sign every day for loans for other people, inevitably subjecting themselves to the dangers of debt.

The internal organs are your financial structure, such as budgeting, saving, and investing. Debt "liquefies" or literally dissolves these things until they are "regurgitated" or given up for the purpose of paying debt.

And lastly, there is the "Ebola seed," the corpse that continues to house the virus, thereby infesting the body and infecting whoever comes in contact with it. In Second Kings 4, the man had died, but by contact through relationship the woman and her sons became infected. If it had not been for the word of the Lord, she too would have suffered. Remember that debt is a contagious disease that wants to destroy you and your whole family.

The Devil's Twin

In John 10:10, Jesus declared that the thief (the devil) comes only to steal, kill, and destroy, but He (Jesus) came that we might have life, and life *more abundantly*. These are two separate things that Jesus promised. First, He promised us life, which is translated as the life of God, or eternal life. But then He said that out of that life there was going to be an abundance. The thief's purpose is to rob us of both of these elements: the life of God and His abundance of blessings.

First Peter 5:8 says that "your adversary the devil, as a roaring lion, walketh about, seeking whom he may devour." Listing the information we have about the devil, we see that he is a thief; his purpose is to steal, kill, and destroy, which is the direct opposite of the purpose of Jesus' coming (keep that in mind); he wants to take our abundance; and he walks subtly (see Gen. 3:1), with the purpose of devouring his captives. When we compare this list to the characteristics of debt, we find striking similarities.

Debt is subtle, walking around to see whom it may devour by means of interest payments and overspending. Its goal is to steal your wealth and resources, kill you spiritually through worry and anxiety, and destroy your spiritual life. *Debt is backed by a powerful spirit of deception, which seduces its victims with temporary pleasure at the cost of permanent bondage.* It is a direct enemy to the will of God for our lives and is totally opposed to the purposes of Christ. Therefore, *the only difference between debt and the devil is that the devil can't get any bigger*! **Debt is the visible manifestation of an invisible devil!**

Christ has accomplished in the spiritual what we need to accomplish in the natural. He defeated the devil in His life in every area, and He paid all the debt we owed from sin (see Col. 2:14-15). Therefore, if we are to be in the image and likeness of God, then *debt has to be defeated in our lives! **Though Jesus has defeated the devil, He has left us with the task of defeating debt.*** Just as Jesus brought the devil to an open shame, so we should do the same with debt because it's the devil's twin.

An Enemy to the Will of God

Debt's goal is to keep us from *finding, fulfilling,* and *furthering* God's will for our lives and His Kingdom on earth. Debt aborts destiny and purpose. Consider that before an abortion takes place, there had to be a conception. God has impregnated everyone with His will. But debt can become so overwhelming that people throw their hands up in surrender and don't even try to defeat it. Though they ignore the problem and want to kill it off, the debt still exists, constantly draining their money and aborting their will until they are total slaves to its power.

Debt knows that if you don't *find* the will of God, you will not reach your potential, for *your purpose contains your potential.* Rather, you will be unproductive and wander aimlessly through life because it takes regular, quality time with God to know His will.

Debt also desires to rob you of your worship by causing you to worry, thus killing any intimacy with God that you may have. Many times people are so busy working, trying to pay off their debts, that they neglect their spiritual development.

When we find God's will but can't fulfill it, two things happen. First, we can't possess the inheritance that comes from the will. God has willed certain things to His children. After His will is identified, we must meet the requirements in order for the trustee, who is the Holy Ghost (see Jn. 14:26; 16:7), to release the inheritance.

Secondly, we become poor stewards. If we know what plan God has for us, but due to *our* circumstances that *we* created we can't fulfill His will, then we are poor stewards. When we can't further the will of God on earth, we become like the unprofitable servant in Matthew 25:14-30. Because he didn't invest the money to further the master's purpose, his master called him wicked. The Greek word for wicked means "one who has failed the Lord in service." Whenever we can't further God's will and purpose in our lives and on the earth, we fail Him in service.

God has entrusted treasures and time to all of us. Debt is out to steal both of them. The money that you pay monthly from being in debt robs you of your treasure and steals opportunities that you would otherwise have had to invest the money to further the Kingdom of God. Additionally, debt causes you to work extra hours to pay things off. This is separate from the time you waste worrying about your debt. *In its fullest form, debt is a visible manifestation of an invisible devil that wants to keep you from the will of God.*

A Premature Withdrawal

In Proverbs 19:14, the Bible says that "house and riches are the inheritance of fathers...." However, debt causes a premature withdrawal from your children's inheritance, and the money that is designed to be passed on to them is instead passed to your creditors.

In Nehemiah chapter 5, the Bible says that there was a cry among the people about the Jews who were oppressing them despite the fact that they were all related. The people had run out of money and were forced to mortgage their houses and land (the children's inheritance) to pay off taxes and have money for food. Some of their children were even sold off as slaves just to meet the basic necessities of life.

Debt has robbed children of their house and riches due to a premature withdrawal made *by their parents*. When a Christian is guilty of poor stewardship, debt presents itself as the only available option, and says, "Slavery is the only choice left to rectify the situation." *But these people went into debt and still didn't have enough.* Debt robbed the children of their inheritance, and the parents still were in no better position than they were beforehand.

Anytime you prematurely withdraw money from an account (e.g., a CD or a retirement fund), a penalty must be paid. Parents penalize themselves when they are unable to contribute to their children's success. The people in Nehemiah 5 were being sold to their creditors and most of the money that they made was going to their slave masters; therefore, their income was not increasing and their children's inheritance was being reduced. Are you making premature withdrawals from your children's inheritance?

Modern-Day Slave Master

It is your economic condition, not the color of your skin or your cultural or ethnic background, that determines your level of freedom. The Bible says in Proverbs 22:7b that "the borrower is servant [slave] to the lender." Debt is a twentieth-century slave master that desires to keep you in bondage. Its power is in enticing deception that leads to a responsibility you cannot forsake.

Debt forces you to work almost inhumanely. In Exodus 1:13-14, we see how the Israelite slaves were treated by their masters. The Bible says that the Israelites had to serve "with rigour" and that "their lives" were "bitter" due to the "hard bondage" of slavery. When in debt, vacation days are usually fewer and work becomes less enjoyable. In the Old Testament, even slaves were not required to work on the Sabbath (see Ex. 20:10). However, twentieth-century slavery desires, and in many cases requires, that you work on the Sabbath so that debt's appetite can be fed.

Debt has no reverence for God; in fact, its goal is to pull you further away from Him (see previous sections). Debt knows that the more hours you work, the more money you make, which allows you to spend more, and thus get in debt even deeper. When the Egyptians came into power, they placed over the Israelites "taskmasters to afflict them with their burdens" (Ex. 1:11), or to give them excessive work and monitor that it was being done. The purpose was to stop the multiplication of the Israelites in Egypt. Debt doesn't want you to multiply your money, for it knows, like the Egyptians, that if there is multiplication, then there is the potential that it could be defeated and removed from power.

Consider David and Goliath. When Goliath made his challenge (see 1 Sam. 17:1-10), the terms were that the Philistines would be slaves to the Israelites and serve them if David won, and the Israelites would be slaves to the Philistines if Goliath won. *See your debt as Goliath and understand that it can take on only one of two roles: servant or master.*

If you defeat debt and it becomes your servant, then it serves you by releasing money for investments, savings, or attacking other debt. However, if you are overtaken by debt, then you become its slave and are subject to a life of hard work with little reward. *Debt's only responsibility (just like a real slave master) is to provide you with the basics (food, clothing, and shelter) so that you can be fit to work.*

Effects of slavery

The repercussions of debt are devastating. Here is a list of some of the most serious ones.

1. *Debt divides the family.* In the Bible, family members were often sold as compensation for unpaid debts, causing the family to be divided forever. This same division is seen today when people are forced to work long hours, sacrificing time with their families and driving a wedge between parents and children.

2. *Debt causes you to live in fear because you lose control over your life.* Slaves never knew what their master was doing or thinking. They had no clue as to whether or not they were going to be sold away from their family, what would happen to their daughters and sons, or even if they would live to see the next day. When in debt, interest rates and fees (e.g., late fee, over-the-limit fee) can accrue without your knowing it. Just as the slave had no control over his life, so debt takes control over your life. This causes many people to be afraid to open their mail or answer the phone.

3. *Debt robs you of your dreams and plans.* Because debt is your master, all your dreams, goals, and plans are subject to it. It tells you what is feasible, what is affordable, and what is not, based on its agenda, not God's.

4. *You are forced to work hard for little or no reward.* Though you have worked full time, you aren't rewarded in proportion to your labor. Slaves were forced to work extremely hard but could enjoy only a small portion of their labor. Debt coupled with interest takes much of what you've worked for and allows you to enjoy only a portion of it.

5. *You own nothing.* Slaves were never allowed to own anything. Debt never allows *you* to own anything. Things are

usually obtained by renting (e.g., apartment instead of house), using credit or a mortgage.

Why would someone want to stay in slavery? In earlier centuries, the loyalty of the slave was based on his treatment. Those slaves who lived in the master's house and had close relationship with the family were usually more loyal than slaves who worked outside the house.

Even the Bible shows us that Solomon's servants were privileged to be his servants because of their treatment (see 1 Kings 10:8). However, they were still servants. In the parable of the prodigal son, the son who wasted his inheritance came back because he remembered the condition of his father's servants and how well they lived. In the Scripture, he proclaimed that he would ask his father to make him a servant. He was choosing slavery because of his unhappiness in his present condition (see Lk. 15:14-19). For people who are not experiencing the prosperity of God, debt presents itself as an option at the expense of their freedom.

In that same parable, the Bible says that after the son had spent all his inheritance, the famine came (see verse 14). Debt lurks in the shadows, waiting for the poor steward to waste his goods so that it can offer itself as an option and recruit another slave. Christians choose to stay in debt because they don't see a better life for themselves or have any hope of being debt-free. In short, debt has robbed them of their faith. (See "Effects and ramifications" earlier in this chapter.)

On the other hand, many Christians just like being in debt. In Exodus 21:5-6, God dealt with Moses on procedures for what to do if a slave wanted to remain a slave even after his time of service was up. People many times do the same thing. As soon as a bill is paid off, instead of moving on to establish more ownership for the Kingdom, they take out another loan and extend their period as a slave. Usually this is because all the person knows is a life of slavery. There are people reading this book who have been in debt for so many years that it would literally be abnormal for them not to owe anyone. If that is you, and you are ever to get out of debt, you may be tempted to get back in debt just to have the feeling of owing someone because that's all you know.

Slavery was a common practice all throughout history. However, widespread slavery (debt) is considered by many historians as one of the chief reasons for the downfall of the Roman Empire. Could debt potentially be the cause of ours? The government says no, because debt stimulates the economy. However, with the economy due for a recession any year now, there will be many people enslaved (in debt) for whom the master will not be able to provide. To everyone in slavery, the time to escape is now. Get out while you can!

Chapter 3

The Purpose of Debt: What Debt Is After

From our own studies and personal experience, we have identified eight things in life that debt has put in its battle plan to destroy. In Chapter 2 we described debt as being the devil's twin. John 10:10 tells us that the devil (thief) comes to *steal, kill,* and *destroy.* We see debt doing the same thing.

God created debt, and everything that He created has a purpose. God's original purpose for debt was to help a neighbor in need without charging interest (see Deut. 15:6-11). However, like most things, it has been perverted to oppress the masses for the benefit of the few.

The perverted purpose of debt is to rob you in eight areas that make up every aspect of your life. If the enemy succeeds in destroying just one of these, your life will be drastically affected. If he destroys or affects all of them, then you are destined for destruction, and no finance company, bank, credit union, or wealthy family member can help you. God's grace and mercy will be your only hope of recovery.

1. Worship

The highest call of any believer is the call to worship. John 4:24 says, "God is a Spirit: and they that worship Him must worship Him in spirit and in truth." In order for someone to worship effectively, he must be focused on the Father. Isaiah 26:3 says, "Thou wilt keep him in perfect peace, whose mind is stayed on Thee: because he trusteth in Thee." However, debt robs you of your focus on God.

During praise and worship, instead of thinking on the Father, people's minds tend to wander and focus on their past due Visa bill, an overdue phone bill, or a late house payment. *Because they have lost focus, they have lost their worship.* Additionally, because your mind is not on Him, you lose *perfect* peace. Though you may have peace for a moment, the enemy comes and steals it because it is not the peace of God. Therefore, it's imperfect.

The success of our life centers around our ability to worship. It is in this intimate time spent with the Father that dreams and goals are birthed. Debt seeks to perform an abortion on your dreams so that they never become a reality. Its method of abortion is to steal your worship. Why? Because worship gets you in the presence of God, and Jesus said that without Him, we could do nothing (see Jn. 15:5).

When debt takes your worship, it becomes your god because it takes God's glory and transfers it to itself. In Psalm 67:5-7, the psalmist declares that when the people praise God, the earth will yield its increase. When debt attacks our worship life, it poisons the ground that our seed is planted in and destroys the earth's potential to yield its increase. Remember that the thief (debt) comes to steal, kill, and destroy, not just your life, but also your seed of worship.

2. Will

It takes gasoline for a car to get from one point to another. Your will is the gasoline that gets you to the place that God wants you to be. It is the motivational factor that propels you to your destiny. Debt is like a siphoning hose that "sucks" your motivation out until your will is broken and you stop caring about anything (e.g., God, bills, work, appearance, etc.). You lose focus of everything that matters because any additional pressure is magnified.

Debt is like an ancient Chinese torture method, where they would lay a prisoner under dropping water. Though the water would fall only one drop at a time, it always fell in the same place with consistency. This would drive a prisoner crazy and break his will to live. It would drive him to the point where he would rather die than continue in that torture.

That's how debt destroys your will. Though small in the beginning, its attack is relentless and consistent, totally breaking down your will to the point where you stop caring about everything. Dams don't break from one huge blast of water. There is consistent water pressure before the dam actually breaks, and before the breaking there is a cracking.

Many people reading this book have had their will cracked by debt and are on the verge of having it broken. When debt begins to destroy your will, you say things like, "Let them come and repossess everything; I don't care!" Your attitude becomes one of hopelessness and despair, and, like a slave (see Chapter 2), you become broken with no drive to fight. *Your dreams of prosperity turn to nightmares of poverty and you become a master of "just making it."*

3. Witness

Why would sinners get saved if they can't see that salvation making a difference in other Christians' lives? The Bible is clear on the importance of financial organization and stewardship, and it is our job to make the Word flesh, or to make it tangible so sinners can see and long for salvation. Debt destroys our witness because it makes salvation unattractive by giving the appearance that the devil is winning.

If an unsaved person can pay his bills on time, love his wife, have good family relationships, and have an abundance in finances, your witness is powerless if you can't at least match his productivity—although you should surpass it. Why? Because you make God look unnecessary. When in debt, creditors see your personal life on profile and determine the potency of the Word by the effect it has on you. Therefore, they can't receive your saying that God will make a difference in their lives when they're wondering when He's going to make a difference in yours.

Many times the "Jesus loves you" on our checks is stamped over by "NSF" by the bank. Which do you think stands out to the sinner? Matthew 5:13 talks about salt losing its savor (taste), therefore making it useless. The taste is the effect salt has on what it touches. Debt comes to rob us of our salt, where we won't have any effect on those with whom we have contact. When you go for a loan, the bank pulls up your credit report, *not your contribution statement from church.* When the loan officer sees it infested with debt (and late payments), your witness loses power outside of the grace of God. ***While we have attacked the devil with our giving, his counter punch of debt has sent many Christians reeling.***

Many times Christians try to defeat natural enemies with spiritual warfare. Although there is an element of spiritual warfare that is important to our victory, there are natural issues that need to be dealt with before God will manifest deliverance. Revelation was practical in Jesus' teaching. It needed to be applied naturally so that people could get deliverance and provision for their situation. Our witness is not empowered by our revelations, but by our testimony (see Rev. 12:11). ***Christians must understand that their credit report is written verification of their integrity.***

What testimony of Christ does your credit report give? When a creditor looks at your credit report, he should be able to tell when you got saved. For example, say that from January 1, 1990, to August 15, 1995, you as an unsaved man or woman always paid your bills late. After you got saved in August, the late payments should stop. From that point on there should be a consistent effort to build a track record of on-time payments that should continue after you are caught up. Eventually the debt should be paid off. *If your payment history chronicled your life, would the date of your salvation be obvious?*

4. Wealth

Debt takes your money! Need we say more? Although wealth is one of the most obvious things that debt wants to take, it is also the hardest loss to stop. Debt steals your wealth from you through finance charges, interest payments, and late penalties.

For example, the majority of a house payment goes to the payment of interest and not to the cost of the house in the early years. On a $100,000 loan at 9 percent, the payment would be approximately $800 (principal and interest). Of that $800, approximately $700 of each payment for the first year goes to interest. Debt knows that a lack of money is part of a curse, and it limits the resources that can advance the Kingdom of God (see Hag. 1:4-10 TLB; Mal. 3:9-11).

When your money is gone, you lose your effectiveness because instead of focusing on God, you focus on your lack of money. (See "Worship" earlier in this chapter.) Being broke and in debt causes frustration and keeps you discouraged. When people become *discouraged* (*dis*, "without"; *courage*, "the conquest of fear"), they stay in fear of opening their mail, seeing their statements, answering the phone, or negotiating payments of old debts. You are *forced* to work overtime or to obtain a part-time job to make ends meet.

In Haggai 1, the Bible speaks of putting your money into pockets with holes. This was because the people put their money into their house instead of sowing it into the Kingdom of God. When you're in debt, you do the same thing. Because all your money goes to *your* debt and *your* living expenses, you "can't afford" to sow. Thus you work for much but gain little. Consider that you now have two powers working against your money:

Interest is eating it away and God is blowing it away. In that situation, you can't afford *not* to sow.

When cash is short, you feel forced to use more credit cards, which in turn creates more debt. At this point, you have been caught by the debt trap (see Chapter 1). When debt takes your wealth, it limits and sometimes strips you of your ability to provide for your family, which causes low self-esteem. Many men have been robbed of their manhood because of their inability to provide for their family due to the effects of debt. Because of this, our society deals with divided homes, high divorce rates, adultery, massive depression, and even suicide—all because debt has taken our wealth.

5. Weapon

The devil sees what most Christians don't see. When most Christians see a $100 bill, all they see is *$100*. The devil sees the $100 bill as a seed (weapon) that has the ability to produce at least a 30-fold and possibly a 100-fold return—and this scares him! If we are going to declare war on debt, we must have a weapon. The weapon that we have in this battle against debt is our seed. ***Debt understands that a seed has the ability to reproduce when it is available and is sown.***

By giving to God through our local church (see Lk. 6:38), to our pastor (see 1 Cor. 9:7-12; Phil. 4:15-19), to other believers (see Prov. 11:24-25), or to the poor (see Prov. 19:17), we allow our seed to be multiplied. When you use the weapon of your seed, your army against debt increases. (One of the definitions of the Hebrew word for "wealth" in the Old Testament is "army" [see Deut. 8:18].) Therefore, debt's strategy is to take your seed by destroying your wealth. (See "Wealth" earlier in this chapter.) If you can't sow your seed, it can't reproduce, which in turn limits the power you have to fight back against your debt.

Your seed is designed by God to advance the Kingdom (see Prov. 10:16 TLB) and to help others (see Deut. 15:6-11). In Second Corinthians 9:10-12, Paul says that doing this "causeth through us thanksgiving to God." When we sow into other people's lives, we cause them to praise God and cause God to move on our behalf. Sowing our seed into those who have less than we do guarantees a return (see Prov. 19:17). Therefore, debt takes our seed to constrict its growth and weaken our attack.

A seed exemplifies God as being a provider. When we sow into other people's lives, we are used by God to express Him in the earth. When we have no seed, God can't use us to express His ability to provide in the earth. *Your money (seed) is your life. You work hours of your life for money; therefore, when you give your money, you give your life.* This shows Christ, who gave His life.

We have the opportunity to *give* our lives while debt wants to *take* our lives. When debt takes your seed, instead of its being used to destroy the works of the devil by supporting missions or building churches, it is used to support the things of the world and so works against you. That which was to be passed on to the next generation of believers has been passed on to heathens. Instead of empowering our kids, we're impoverishing them. The goal of debt is to render you defenseless so that it might eventually destroy you.

6. Warfare

In First Timothy 6:11-12, Paul tells Timothy to "fight the good fight of faith" and "lay hold on eternal life" because that is what he and every other believer has been called to. In other words, every believer has a right to eternal life, but he or she must fight for it. We have already been promised the victory, *so the enemy tries to prevent us from coming to fight.*

When we are swamped with debt, we lose our will to "fight the good fight," and consequently we become defeated. When we are consumed with two and three jobs to make ends meet, we become too busy to fight and are entangled with the affairs of the world (see 2 Tim. 2:4). This causes warfare and intimacy with God to become secondary to paying our bills.

A minister who came to our church once said that the biggest problem in the Church's fulfilling its vision is not the devil, for God has already defeated him. Rather, it's debt. Debt constricts our will to pray, intercede, study our Bible, and do the natural things that prepare us to be used by God.

Remember that the Israelites refused to fight the giants in the wilderness because of their size (see Num. 13:27-33). When they considered how big their problem was, they lost their will to fight. Many times when we look at our debt, it appears so insurmountable that we lose our will to fight and consequently are banished to the wilderness for an extended stay.

God told the children of Israel to search the land to test whether or not they believed that they could possess it. By their rebellion *and* delay they were defeated by the enemy. Notice that when they were rebuked, they tried to go and possess the land anyway and were destroyed. Why? They were not backed by the word of the Lord. We have a word that "whatsoever we do will prosper" (see Ps. 1:3); "God shall supply all of our need" (see Phil. 4:19); and "we can do all things through Christ" (see Phil. 4:13). However, when we get consumed with the cares of the world, that word is choked and becomes ineffective (see Mk. 4:18-19). You are distracted from the real issues of life by continuously worrying and wondering about your future.

Debt's goal is to confuse you in the battle of life so that you can be defeated. Confused people see everything from an erroneous viewpoint. ***Eventually you begin to war against creditors and your spouse, ignoring the real enemy, the devil.*** Debt has turned you against yourself and your closest ally (spouse), for it knows that a divided kingdom (house) will eventually fall (see Mt. 13:25).

7. Worth

One of our biggest motivational factors is how we feel about ourselves. The less that we feel we're worth, the less we'll invest in ourselves. When attacked by debt, many times we believe the opposite of what God said about us.

In Deuteronomy 15:6, God tells the Israelites that He will make good on His promise of blessing them after the Abrahamic blessing (see Gen. 12:1-3) and that they will lend to and reign over many nations. Debt wants to choke the Word (see "Warfare" earlier in this chapter) and get you to believe contrary to the promise: "I'll *never* be blessed; I'm *cursed*!" Debt makes it seem like God doesn't care about you, for if He did, He wouldn't have allowed this to happen. You feel ashamed, worthless, embarrassed, and confused. You lose faith in yourself and the God in you. Eventually, you see God no differently than you see yourself.

However, we forget that our condition is a result of *our* decisions. People (especially men and parents) lose their sense of worth when they desire to give their wife and children the basics of life but can't.

Debt eventually affects your family name. Proverbs 22:1 states that the worth of your name is more important than the amount of material possessions you have. When a man has a good name, he has favor with both God and man, which is necessary for success. Though Moses had favor with God, he couldn't get the children of Israel out of Egypt until he got favor with Pharaoh. Favor will get you places where money can't.

Debt looks to destroy your name, and ultimately your favor with man. Banks usually don't favor a man who has more debt than income and is late in paying his bills. Creditors are less lenient with someone who has a poor payment history. Your name has direct impact on your future and helps to determine your worth to others. Regardless of your present situation, however, you're valuable and have worth to God; you're His child.

8. Work

Webster's Dictionary defines work as "physical or mental activity undertaken to achieve a purpose involving the expenditure of effort." Everything has a purpose and *although debt doesn't destroy your ability to work, it does redirect its purpose from gainful employment to slavery.* (See Chapter 1, "Slavery.")

Keep in mind the story of David and Goliath and the arrangement made by Goliath beforehand (see 1 Sam. 17:8-9). The outcome of the battle determined the purpose of work for a nation. And the outcome of your battle with debt will determine the purpose of work for your nation (family). The time that God has called you to spend *developing* your ministry gift and discovering your purpose is consumed because you are a servant to debt's purpose and are constantly working.

Imagine if you never fulfilled the purpose or work that God has called you to do (because you don't find it). The people whom God had predestined you to reach won't be reached and could potentially be locked in hell for eternity—all because debt robbed you of your time to discover your work here in the earth.

You hold the dollar that makes the difference in whether your church builds their new outreach facility or not, but it goes to debt. The person whom you were supposed to meet at an entrepreneurial convention and later marry, you never meet, and so you have to settle for God's backup plan. And finally, the inheritance that your children would have used to go to college and start a business empire and dynasty, they never receive—all because of debt. Debt affects far more than just you; it affects people and generations to come. *It robs God's providence of its potency and leaves you wandering instead of achieving.*

To be a servant to the purpose of debt makes you an enemy to the purpose of God (see Mt. 12:30). God can't trust His enemies with the keys to the Kingdom (see Mt. 16:13-21); therefore, the wealth that is laid up for you becomes unattainable (see Prov. 13:22). When you're overloaded with debt, the desire for ministry is gone because all your energy is exhausted by fighting debt. Remember that debt is only one of many tactics used by the devil, and if all your energy is exerted in fighting debt and trying to meet your needs, how can you meet the needs of others?

Chapter 4

The Personality of Debt: What Debt Is Like

In Chapter 2, we dealt with the **person** of debt (who and what debt is). In this chapter, we will look at debt's **personality** (what debt is like). Every person has a personality directly related to who he or she is. Debt's person and personality are *directly related*, but they are *not* the same. Regardless of its bad traits, *debt is focused, goal-oriented, and driven by purpose—that's why it is so successful.* Therefore, in order to defeat debt we must know its personality, which will in turn reveal to us more about its purpose and help us keep debt in proper perspective in our lives.

Deceptive

In John 8:44, Jesus declared that the devil is the father of all lies. Since we know that debt is directly related to the devil as one of his attacks, we know that debt is full of lies. Debt will tell you that you can pay it off when you get paid or when the statement comes, only to have an unforeseen expense arise and take the money that you had purposed for the debt. Debt makes no mistake about its ability, but it will tell *you* that you can handle multiple credit cards, which are its master tools for acquiring slaves. (See Chapter 1, "Slavery.")

Debt deceives by convincing its victims that a minimum payment is enough to control it. It does not tell you that interest lurks in the shadow to multiply your mistakes. The power of debt's deception is so great that it tricks you into committing the same mistake again by getting you to think that circumstances are different.

Just as "Satan himself masquerades as an angel of light" (2 Cor. 11:14 AMP), so debt deceives the Body of Christ into thinking that it is the road to prosperity. *Slavery (debt) never leads to divine prosperity unless it is God appointed.* (Read Joseph's story in Genesis 37–41.) Although debt may provide an initial springboard for you to achieve your goals, its ramifications always outrun your progress and eventually overtake you.

Every motive of debt has a deceptive edge. In understanding debt, we must keep in mind its overall purpose, which is to steal, kill, and destroy. Debt is full of promises that it cannot keep. Debt is not designed to lead, but to overtake and redirect all efforts toward its purpose.

Nothing that debt tells you can be taken as true. For example, if you are expecting an income tax refund check for $500 to come in two weeks, you might go and buy a $200 dress, a $100 pair of shoes, and spend the rest on the town (all on credit) with the *intent* of paying the debt when the check comes. Notice that all this spending was done *before* the check was actually received and nothing was mentioned about an offering. *Most people think that if the money hasn't been received, then it shouldn't be tithed on. If that's true, then it shouldn't be spent either. What you can do for yourself in advance, you can do for God in advance.*

Because of these factors, an unforeseen expense will usually arise and the money that you had allotted to debt must be redirected. You just went into weeks of slavery for a dress, some shoes, and one night out. You have been *played* and "*pimped*" by your own desires and incontinency. It's obvious that you couldn't afford what you bought because you had to rely on a credit card and an income tax refund to purchase it. Debt has succeeded in deceiving you about even your *own* abilities, all for its devious purpose.

As you familiarize yourself with debt, it gets you to introduce it to your children at a young age by signing a letter of intent (a credit card application) so that they can be its slave in future years. Debt's deception allows it to present itself as a way out of trouble, a friend in the time of need, a supplier of your needs, and a way to your desires. All these are actually characteristics of Jesus (see Ps. 46:1; Heb. 4:16; Phil. 4:19; Mk. 11:24). Debt has fulfilled Second Corinthians 11:13-14 as a "financial false apostle," appearing to be sent from God, but whose actual assignment is to deceive and destroy the Church.

Destructive

When Jesus spoke of the devil's threefold purpose in John 10:10, He spoke of a gradual process. The devil wants to first take your possessions, then take your life, both spiritually and physically. Finally, he wants to destroy any trace of your existence. Debt has the same goals.

After debt steals your wealth and kills your vision, it wants to destroy your legacy. The Bible says that a good man leaves an inheritance (e.g., houses and riches, according to Proverbs 19:14) for his future generations (see Prov. 13:22). Debt wants to rob you of the resources that make it possible for you to leave an inheritance, and therefore destroy any trace of your existence. Nothing is left as a memorial to your accomplishments.

In Second Kings 4:1-4, the woman's husband was a prophet of God who spoke the word of the Lord and probably brought deliverance to many. Unfortunately, the only memorial that he had was one of debt and desolation, to the point that his family was *minutes* away from slavery.

Things that have been stolen or killed can be returned or resurrected, but when something is destroyed, it cannot be recovered. In John 17:12, Jesus tells the Father that the only one He couldn't keep was Judas, the "son of perdition [destruction]." Therefore Judas was destined to be lost. The ultimate goal of debt is to get our finances into such a state of destruction that not even God can resurrect them.

Some say, "But God can do anything!" Keep in mind that God has not created anything new since Genesis 1. Everything has evolved from the initial creation, and God has chosen to use the existing creation to fulfill His will in the earth. In order for God to resurrect your finances, you need a *seed*.

In First Corinthians 15:36, Paul said that what is sown cannot be quickened, brought to life, or resurrected unless it dies. When a seed (money) is sown, the buying power of that dollar is dead to you. Since it is dead, it can now be resurrected. Debt knows that if you sow a certain amount of money, it will die and qualify for resurrection in a 30-fold or 100-fold harvest. Therefore, debt is out to destroy your seed because what is *destroyed* cannot be resurrected!

Debt wants to destroy your worship, will, witness, wealth, weapon, warfare, worth, and work. (See Chapter 3.) It also wants to destroy your relationships (e.g., family, friends), your health, your dreams, and your goals. Therefore, just as it is important for us not to "give place to the devil" (Eph. 4:27), so we should not give place to debt to destroy our lives.

Domineering

In the story of David and Goliath, the deal that Goliath made was that the winner of the battle would give his nation *dominion* over the nation of the loser. Many Christians are losing or have already lost the battle with debt. Consequently, debt has taken dominion over them.

Debt must always be in control in order to have full effect. When you have a debt, you are sent a monthly statement that is nothing more than an ultimatum. It says that if you don't pay your creditors what you owe as well as meet their demands (called interest), then they will punish you. By going into debt, you have given your creditors total dominion over your life where they can take money from you without your permission. (It's known to us as interest.) They also determine who loans you money in the future and at what rate. In this way debt gains monopolistic control over your giving to your church, your place of residence, your feelings, the time that you spend with your family, and even the time that you spend with God!

Debt's nature is to dominate. *When debt is not dominating, it literally changes its identity from that of a debt to an investment.* Therefore, without dominion debt has no future! Debt is like a school yard bully. The bully will pick on you as long as he can sense your fear and you don't fight back. But as soon as you make up your mind that you aren't going to be bullied anymore, you have the courage to attack. Usually after *you* fight back, the bully doesn't bother you anymore (but he will bother others).

When we make up our minds that we are not going to be bullied by debt anymore, we gain the courage it takes to face our bills and mount an attack. And just like a bully, after you attack debt, you'll see that it isn't as tough to overcome as you thought. *The key is getting the courage to attack.*

Relentless

Debt mounts an attack that starts off slow and gentle, but will eventually turn fierce and relentless. After catching you in the debt trap (see Chapter 1), debt will bombard you with seductive ads and opportunities to create more debt. Offers will include free sign-up gifts, low introductory APR's, no interest for the first year, or deferred payments. What debt does not tell you is the powerful onslaught that you will face after your "grace period."

Debt doesn't take "no" for an answer. It will constantly entice you with deal after deal, stalking you like an old boyfriend or girlfriend until it breaks your will, you give in, and it abuses you.

(See Chapter 3.) Just like a one-night stand with an old flame, the debt acquired from one more loan will have an impact that lasts for years.

Debt will do anything to keep you: reduce the payment, stretch the terms, require no money down, or lower the price. Debt is a fatal attraction that can have lethal consequences. Once it has hooked you, it gets the word out on how "easy" you are to pick up, and tells all its friends (the lending institutions and credit card companies). They begin to call you and send you letters of pre-approval to see if they can get from you the same thing that their friend got—*your money.*

Debt is attracted to your money, and the more you have, the more relentless the attack is. (Credit card companies and loan agencies offer their services most to people with the greatest income.) Don't be deceived and eventually "pimped" by debt! Keep it at a distance, for its attack is persistent and relentless!

Ruthless

A man once had a dream of a person "play fighting" with the devil. As long as the person had the upper hand, both he and the devil kept a playful attitude. However, the devil eventually got the upper hand and pinned the man to the floor. As the man looked up, the expression on the devil's face changed and he said, "We are not playing anymore." At that point the struggle became real.

Debt is the devil's twin—many of their actions are the same. Debt will play with you until it gets the upper hand. At that time the attack becomes relentless and its attitude ruthless. Debt has no pity and is brutal, cruel, and inhumane. Although debt is nice to you when it wants you to borrow more, after you are locked in it accepts no excuses and is only concerned with getting its money *now.*

Debt doesn't care about layoffs, unforeseen expenses, college tuition, or investment opportunities. The sweet, enticing phone calls that lured you into the contract become nasty and abrasive ones. The people who loaned you the money are beginning to reveal their true identity.

Think about the different ways that the devil entices the saints into sin, only to bombard them with guilt and condemnation after the fact. The devil has never let up on his attack. When he's not attacking, he's devising the next attack.

Debt longs to set us up so that it can have total control over our lives and can attack our finances to the point that they are utterly destroyed. At this stage, debt tells you to do whatever you have to do to pay, whether it's cheating on your taxes, cheating on your time card, not paying your tithe and offering, stealing, borrowing, or even making your young kids work.

In Second Kings 4:1-7, the creditors had come to take the woman's children. In other words, they didn't care about her husband's status, her financial condition, or the welfare of her children. All they wanted was compensation for the debt that was owed. Debt doesn't even fear your status as a man or woman of God.

The only power that debt has is what we give it. So, even though we are men and women of God, when we sell our power and authority to debt, we lose our effectiveness in Kingdom issues. Because we have given power over us to debt, it doesn't fear our status. Why? It has some of our power.

Debt ruthlessly takes control of our seed, nullifying our ability to speak to the seed and prophesy a harvest. After debt gets the upper hand and you refuse to cooperate with its plan of actions, it begins to threaten to tell your boss, destroy your credit, and even repossess your possessions. Debt is a two-faced monster that can't be trusted.

Subtle

Webster's Dictionary defines subtle as "hard to grasp, difficult to define or distinguish, elusive." Something that is subtle is difficult to contain. In Genesis 3:1a, the Bible defines the devil as being "more subtle than any beast of the field." In biblical Hebrew, *subtle* means crafty, cunning, or wise.

Remember that the devil and debt are twins. (See Chapter 2.) Therefore, many of their characteristics will be the same. Just as the devil is defined as subtle and crafty, so debt is also. It spies out your weaknesses based on your spending habits and prepares a plan of attack to exploit them. It will offer you more credit because, based on its research, it knows that you will spend 35 percent more with credit than with cash.

Just as the devil made a play on words in Genesis 3:1b ("Yea, hath God said, Ye shall not eat of every tree of the garden?"), *debt plays on the fact that God wants you blessed, deceiving you into thinking that more credit in the midst of existing debt is a blessing.* The Bible says in Proverbs 10:22, "The blessing of the Lord, it maketh rich, and He addeth no sorrow with it." *If God blessed you with more credit, then He has a responsibility to bless you with the resources to pay off the debt. If that's not provided, then the credit was not of God and debt has set you up to destroy your finances.*

Notice that the devil approached Eve at her point of need with a beautiful appearance. Usually debt presents itself as a savior for our situation; however, it really desires to sink us into bondage. Right at the time of an unexpected expense, the holidays, vacation, or kids going back to school, debt offers a credit card to take care of it. Just like the situation between the devil and Eve, the plan works, unless we know its intentions beforehand.

When debt has "beguiled" us (see Gen. 3:13), the impact lasts for generations. Adam and Eve were thrown out of the Garden of Eden, or Paradise, because they were deceived by the enemy. When we are deceived by debt, it causes us to be thrown out of "Paradise," or to lose the prosperity and lifestyle that God wants us to have. The only way to return to Paradise in our finances is for them to be redeemed.

Finances are redeemed through prayer and repentance, study of the Word (particularly Scriptures on finances), budgeting, goals, and proper stewardship. Consider Psalm 119:9, where David says, "Wherewithal shall a young man cleanse his way? by taking heed thereto according to Thy word." Only then will we see the prosperity of God return to our life and the effects of debt vanish.

Seductive

The word *seductive* means "to cause to wander or lead astray." James 1:14 tells us that men are drawn away by their own lust, and then enticed or seduced. The seduction of debt follows the same process. Debt plays on your needs and desires as bait to draw you away. James 1:15 says, "Then when lust hath conceived, it bringeth forth [gives birth to] sin: and sin, when it is finished [complete, fully matured], bringeth forth [gives birth to] death." As debt draws us away by our own lusts, sin is brought forth by overspending and poor stewardship (e.g., no tithe and offering, late payments, and no budgeting). When overspending and poor stewardship run their course, they give birth to the death of your finances.

Debt will break down your restraint by consistently coming after you with things that you really want (e.g., clothes, computers, cars, etc.), but you know is not the time for you to have. Everyone would like to have new things, take vacations, and eat out. But debt destroys your sense of vision (see Chapter 1), which prevents you from seeing the big picture containing your goals and dreams. *You can only be seduced by something that you want.*

Debt seduces us with "signs and wonders" (see Mk. 13:22) by providing an avenue to obtain new things. Credit cards provide a way to obtain items without cash. The problem is that you sink deeper into bondage with every swipe of the card.

While being seduced, companies tell you how great your credit is and how well you've been paying (or, how good of a slave you are, if you're in debt). They tell you that they don't want to lose you because you are a preferred customer. By playing on your emotions, they get you to buy more things. You feel good buying and spending because they have made you feel like you can handle it. However, you must face what you've "brought forth" or "given birth to" (see Jas. 1:15) when their statements come and you become remorseful. It's too late for an abortion then; you have to handle the responsibility. The steps of seduction are as follows:

1. **The desire.** You want something that is off limits to you *now*.
2. **The contact.** The person (debt) senses your desire.
3. **The words.** They (debts) tell you that you can have what you want without an immediate cost or commitment.
4. **The act.** You get what you've been wanting and you like it! However, you don't consider the cost.
5. **The remorse.** Now you see the cost and the fact that you are trapped.

Keep in mind that the only difference between debt and the devil is that the devil can't get any bigger!

Chapter 5

The Perception of Debt: Misconceptions About Debt

Since the devil is the father of all lies (see Jn. 8:44), and since debt is the devil's twin, then debt will also lie to us and give us a misconception about it so that it can keep its dominion over us. *The root of debt must first be exposed before it can be attacked.* When we get the proper perspective that debt is an enemy to the will of God, then we can prepare a proper battle plan to defeat it.

The purpose of this chapter is to expose some of the lies that debt tells about itself. Many of these misconceptions are learned from family members, the world, or friends. We will identify eight of the most common misconceptions about debt, then give you the truth according to the Word of God to free you from the web of deception that has trapped much of the Body of Christ (see Jn. 8:32).

Misconception #1
"Debt will always be a part of life."

Debt will remain in your life only as long as you allow it to. You must realize that debt is an enemy that can be defeated. Just as the slaves of the eighteenth and nineteenth centuries always hoped for abolition and freedom, so should you hope to be debt-free.

It is imperative that you surround yourself with people who either have become debt-free or are working toward it. The reason that we think debt is a part of life is because everyone we know is in debt and has been for a while. We've seen our parents, friends, church leaders, and even our country, in debt (which is no role model for getting out). The role model for living a debt-free life is Jesus. *He could pay our debt because He had none of His own.*

Proverbs 13:20 says, "He that walketh with wise men shall be wise: but a companion of fools shall be destroyed." This lets us know that the company we keep is prophetic of our destiny. A man once said that an individual is the average of the five people whom he or she hangs around the most. If all your associations are with people who are debt-infested and poor stewards, chances are that you will be the same way.

Test your mind. Would it be more believable if someone said that his family was totally debt-free, or if the family were overwhelmed with debt? The average person believes that people are overwhelmed with debt because that's what we are exposed to the most. Many are like the lame man in John 5, who had given up hope on receiving his healing and considered his condition as a part of life.

On the other hand, there are countless promises in Scripture that point to God's desire for us to be debt-free and have more than enough (see Deut. 15:6; Jn. 10:10; Eph. 3:20; Phil. 4:19). In the Law, the end of seven years was the Lord's release, where every person would release his neighbors of their debt (see Deut. 15:1-2). God is a proponent of being debt-free; therefore, it can't be His will for debt to be a part of our lives.

The government encourages you to be in debt because it helps to stimulate the economy. *You are only one out of 260 million people in the United States. Let the rest of the people stimulate the economy without you and your family.* Your mind must be retrained to get out of thinking that major purchases must be financed and not paid for in cash.

As long as you look to finance your actions with a loan, you will never strive to pay cash. Start by paying cash for small things like food and clothes, then move your way up to bigger things such as furniture and vacations. Finally, pay cash for major purchases like cars, houses, and land. When you live a life infested with debt and co-sign for your children, you perpetuate a cycle of debt and prepare them for a future life of slavery.

Misconception #2
"You attack debt by making more money."

Debt is never accumulated based on how much money you *make*, but by how much money you *spend.* It is your spending habits that affect your financial condition. If you are a person who always spends a portion of your paycheck to buy clothes, making more money would only give you a reason to buy more clothes (see Eccles. 5:9-10). Making more simply gives you the ability to create more debt.

Credit card companies will give greater limits to people with higher incomes. Additionally, people who make more usually feel like they can afford more debt; consequently, they charge more. If a bucket has a hole in it, you don't fix it by filling it with more water. Similarly, when you have a problem in your spending, the problem is not fixed with more money but by reducing your spending.

If you think that debt is based on how much money you make, you are already defeated. If you think that extra money is your only weapon, then you will always have debt in your life. There are three keys to getting out of debt:

1. See debt as a hostile enemy.
2. Control spending. This stops your money leaks.
3. Reduce your cost. You have a greater chance to reduce your spending in the next 30 days than you do of getting a raise.

Debt is a repercussion of overspending rather than a consequence of underpayment. Remember, if you can't identify the problem's root, then you'll never destroy the problem's fruit. You can't use debt to attack debt by borrowing your way out of it. *Debt consolidation without problem elimination creates financial frustration.* Whatever you overspend to get into debt, you'll have to underspend to get out of debt.

Misconception #3
"Debt helps me save on taxes."

We have heard people say that it is a good idea to keep a mortgage on your house in order to get the tax deduction. What if we were to tell you that for every dollar you give us, we will keep it and give you back only 15 cents? Just as no one in his right mind would jump at that opportunity, no one in his right mind should keep an existing debt for a "tax break."

For every dollar that you pay in interest, you get back only *15 cents* as a tax benefit (assuming that, like most people, you're in the 15 percent tax bracket). You have *lost 85 cents* in the transaction. If you paid $10,000 in interest on your home in one year, you would get a $10,000 deduction that saves you *only $1,500* in taxes; however, you would *lose $8,500* to interest. Debt has just tricked you out of almost *six times* what it gave you.

The wise thing to do would be to pay off the house, which would increase your taxes $1,500 per year. However, you would have $10,000 that you didn't have to pay in interest, leaving *you* (not the mortgage company) with $8,500. By keeping debt for tax purposes, you only raise the cost of the product that you are paying on.

Most interest now is not tax deductible (car, credit cards, finance companies, etc.) unless it is for business or charity. The most common deductible interest is mortgage interest, and the tax deduction is not worth going into debt over. There are better ways to save on your taxes. For example, your tithe and offering to your church is a tax deduction, and *it provides you with the same tax benefit as mortgage interest.* Other possible tax deductions include the following:

- Non-cash gifts to charity
- Miles driven for your church
- 401K/403B (retirement plans)
- Money given in Sunday school or to other churches
- Contributions to regular IRA
- Child care so you can work
- Various college credits
- Unreimbursed job expenses

Even business owners can get valuable deductions without going into debt. Examples include these:

- Business use of your home
- Equipment (Per IRC Section 179, it can be expenses in one year. Some limits apply.)
- Miles driven for your business
- Salaries to children (provided that they actually work)
- Travel for business
- Retirement plans (e.g., SEP-IRA)

Don't let ungodly counsel direct the course of your finances (see Ps. 1:1). It is clear that debt is not needed to save in taxes.

Misconception #4
"Credit cards don't cause me to spend more."

Many people feel this way because when they spend with a credit card, they don't feel the loss of cash. Studies show that people spend *35 percent more* with a credit card. Most credit card limits are more money than people actually have to spend. Credit card companies deceive you by convincing you that you can handle the responsibility of the payments. They offer low introductory APR's, no interest for a short period of time, or no annual fees. This is only bait to get you to charge more.

Debt releases an initial feeling of satisfaction and fulfillment, but as time passes and the bills come, the fulfillment turns to regret. When you pay for things with a credit card, you are usually spending money that you don't have. If you had the money, why not pay cash for the item? *Credit cards allow you to spend money that you don't have to get things you don't need to impress people who don't matter.*

The misconception is that the credit limit is the amount that you are supposed to spend. A credit limit is simply rope to hang yourself with. *Your credit card limit is not a spending requirement; it merely represents the maximum amount that the company trusts you with.* An overwhelming desire to have money to spend will never be satisfied (see Eccles. 5:10-11; Prov. 27:20).

Proverbs 21:20 (TLB) says, "The wise man *saves* for the future, but the foolish man spends whatever he gets." By saving, a person doesn't have to charge his needs, wants, or emergency expenses. *Remember, when there is no emergency fund, everything becomes an emergency.* Therefore, people spend all their money, throwing caution to the wind and *forcing* themselves into bondage. When debt becomes your only option, you put your future on hold and extend your stay in your present condition.

Misconception #5
"If I pay the minimum payment on my debt, I'm okay."

Credit card companies and loan institutions make profits off your interest. Therefore, it is in *their* best interest to help you extend the period of your loan. You extend this time when all you pay is the minimum payment on your debt. Interest accrues monthly, which offsets the effect of your payment. *Paying the minimum payment maximizes their profit.*

For example, if you have a credit card balance of $3,000 with an interest rate of 19.8 percent, and no new purchases, the minimum payment requirement is 2 percent of the balance or $15, whichever one is the greatest. If you only pay the minimum payment every month, it would take you 39 years to pay off the balance and you would have paid over *$10,000* in non-deductible interest!

In another example, if you have a $100,000 balance on a house and a 30-year loan with a 9 percent interest rate, you pay over $189,000 in *interest*. However, on a 15-year mortgage the total interest paid is $89,000, *which provides an actual savings* versus the 30-year mortgage. With a 30-year mortgage, the deduction yields only a percentage savings (approximately 15 cents for every dollar). With the 15-year mortgage, you save over $100,000 in *real money*. The deceit is in the tax deduction, which is actually bait for a long, slow death.

An interesting note is that the words *mortgage* and *mortuary* have the same root word. *The tax deduction helps your taxes at the expense of taking your money.* It is just as good in the long run to pay off the debt as it is to carry a mortgage. The problem is that the world literally penalizes you for paying off a debt early. Why? Because it cuts into their profits. Some companies will even take their credit cards from you, and some mortgage companies will charge a prepayment penalty.

When you pay the minimum payment, it creates a tolerance for debt and literally tells it that you expect to see it next month. *The ability to tolerate your present situation creates the inability to change it.*

Misconception #6
"Spending will motivate me, make me happier, and make my life more fulfilling."

We understand that when we don't know something's purpose, we are bound to abuse it. When we don't give purpose to our spending, we abuse it and it eventually becomes our downfall.

Spending abuse is like drug abuse. It provides an initial high while you're doing it, but when you come back down there is depression, guilt, and even condemnation. People who abuse drugs are usually attempting to fill a void in their lives. *Many people spend in an effort to fill a void that was left by God.*

Countless numbers of people attempt to spend their way out of depression. However, spending is the leading cause of debt, which is depression's traveling companion. *It is impossible to spend your way out of debt.* Very rarely do you see a person who is both happy and swamped with debt.

Debt creates an inability to achieve your goals and live out your dreams. Overspending and debt are just like drug addictions: the more you spend, the more you have to spend to get the same high. Spending should never be used as a means of finding happiness. Spending only motivates you to spend more.

In Luke 18:18-24, there is a dialogue between Jesus and a rich young ruler on the subject of eternal life. The ruler had wealth and possessions, yet there was a void in his life that could only be filled by God (hence his question on how to inherit eternal life). His riches and his spending could not provide ultimate happiness and failed to fill the void. Spending to gain material possessions had so gripped his life that he was unwilling to give those possessions up to fulfill his ultimate desire and greatest need.

Many of us, when we see an opportunity to get something that we've always wanted, and realize that it will cost us what we have (e.g., our current habits and lifestyle), will decide to put our dreams on hold. Many would rather enjoy the pleasures of sin for a season than sacrifice their sinful habits for a lifetime of prosperity (see Heb. 11:25).

What you own is not what determines you as a person. Jesus said in Luke 12:15 that "...a man's life consisteth not in the abundance of the things which he possesseth." Nevertheless, people get caught in the cycle of overspending.

Initially, the spending makes you happy. You are excited about your new purchase and are on a "high." As the days go by, you begin to think about the bill coming next month. At this point, worry sets in, especially if you don't know how you're going to pay the bill. When the bill comes, depression sets in. Every bill produces a greater level of depression; therefore, the only two ways to deal with the problem are to match your depression with greater spending, or change your spending habits. Changing your habits is the only true solution to the problem.

Misconception #7
"God is going to perform a miraculous debt cancellation; therefore, I don't have to do anything."

We stated earlier in this chapter that God is a proponent of His people being debt-free (see Lev. 25). However, many Christians have a misconception about the purpose of miracles. The original purpose of miracles was to testify of the power of God; a miracle was a sign to the believers and the heathen. Jesus performed miracles for people who had *done all that they knew to do in their situation*, and in order for the problem to be solved, God had to intervene. Jesus also performed miracles because of the people's lack of faith and obedience (see Mk. 4:35-41; Jn. 2:1-12).

Although it is possible that God may do a miraculous debt cancellation, you must *qualify* for the miracle. God will not help you to get out of debt if you don't pay tithes and give offerings, save money, follow a budget, and cut some of your spending. *If you are not willing to change your current habits, God is not willing to change your current situation. God is only responsible to pay for what He authorizes.*

Many times we make unauthorized purchases with our cash and credit cards ("by faith") and expect God to pay for them miraculously. An unauthorized purchase is any unnecessary, unplanned purchase that has nothing to do with God's plan and purpose for your life. One of the main reasons that people make unauthorized, unnecessary purchases is because they don't know their purpose.

If you asked a person to do a specific task, such as to clean your carpet, you would be responsible for providing anything that was necessary for that person to clean your carpet. Therefore, if he were to come and ask you for carpet cleaner, you would have no problem providing it because it is necessary to complete the task. However, if he were to come and ask you for a *TV Guide* magazine or a Nintendo game, you would more than likely deny the request because it has nothing to do with completing the assigned task.

As crazy as it sounds to ask for a *TV Guide* when the assignment is to clean the carpet, many of the requests God's children
make to Him are just as crazy. The key to proper spending and
getting God to back your purchases and pay for your debts is
knowing your purpose, then praying and purchasing based on it.

The reason God blessed Israel with the things of the Egyptians and canceled their debts was because they needed the things
they received to fulfill His purpose in going to the Promised
Land. Being in debt for the items would have kept them in a type
of bondage and continued their ties with the Egyptians.

When we make unauthorized purchases, we strain ourselves
and hinder our faith. *Remember, your faith will work, but it won't
do the work you are to do.* Faith will never do what work, planning, and stewardship are designed to do. James 2:17 declares,
"Even so faith, if it hath not works, is dead, *being alone.*" **Faith
can never stand on its own. It must be accompanied by something or it will die.**

The life-support system of your faith is action. Therefore, if
you have faith in God to deliver you from debt's choke hold, you
must put forth the action that confirms your faith. *If God were to
cancel your debt without you putting forth any effort, it would
make you irresponsible.* The process is needed to mature you and
help you develop a hatred of debt.

Misconception #8
"I can borrow my way out of debt."

Trying to borrow your way out of debt is like trying to eat
more to lose weight. It is a contradiction of terms, and it generally defeats the purpose of the effort. Just like some diets say that
you can "pig out to a slimmer you," some people say that you can
borrow your way out of debt. However, doing that only spreads
the disease and potentially prolongs your stay in slavery (debt).

Many times, new companies will offer lower interest rates on
credit cards or debt consolidation. Although this can be good, if
the root of your debt problem is not exposed and dealt with,

you've created additional credit limits and potentially greater debt. *The key to getting out of debt is discipline.*

Borrowing from creditors to get out of debt is just another attempt to find a "quick fix" in a situation without dealing with the actual issue. Consequently, you will repeat the same process and mistake. Proverbs 26:11 says, "As a dog returneth to his vomit, so a fool returneth to his folly." Therefore, if the actual cause of the problem is not dealt with, you are bound to repeat it.

Chapter 6

The Process: Why People Get in Debt

Most people don't acquire uncontrollable debt overnight. Debt begins as an attitude and is cultivated by poor money management habits. Its process is methodical and feeds off the character traits of the individual. We are going to look at some of the common reasons why people get into debt and the effect that it has on their finances and lives.

Greed

In Proverbs 30:8-9, Agur asks that the Lord remove all vanity and lies from him and that He give him neither poverty nor riches. He feared that, being rich, he would deny the Lord and find Him unnecessary; and that, being poor, he would be tempted to steal and take the name of God in vain. Agur knew that being consumed by either condition would potentially lead to greed in his life.

Greed is desiring more than God intended for you to have. The reason so many people get caught in greed is because they

don't know their purpose. (See Chapter 5, "Misconception #7.")
When people don't know their purpose, they don't know what
they need to fulfill it.

Greed is one of the most powerful desires known to man. The
Bible says in Proverbs 27:20, "Hell and destruction are never full;
so the eyes of man are never satisfied." The more your flesh gets,
the more it wants. Therefore, trying to satisfy it is vain and will
only lead you into greed.

Greed will cause you to take all you can get without consid-
eration for your family, friends, church, or any *needs* that you
may have. Every day people go to malls, department stores, grocery stores, and clothing stores to purchase things that they want
but don't need. It is nothing for a woman to have 100 pairs of
shoes or a man to have 50 ties in their wardrobe. Although every
person in that category could try to give reasons for why so many
shoes or ties are necessary, very few people need that many.
These are perfect examples of greed. It's not that the person needed the shoes or the ties; they just wanted them.

Your flesh will always want new shoes, clothes, cars, etc., but
it becomes greed when you sacrifice your necessities and the
needs of others to get what you want, throwing caution to the
wind and stopping at nothing to fulfill your desires. *When the
value of your clothes exceeds the value of your savings, your
upkeep just became your downfall.*

Remember, debt never says *spend less*; it always says *make
more.* The goal of greed is to get you to look successful before
you are successful, which is a form of deception (one of the characteristics of debt). Greed is one of the leading causes of debt and
until you bring your flesh under subjection (see 1 Cor. 9:27), you
will always be enslaved by the power of greed and debt.

Desire for New Things

There is nothing wrong with a desire for new things; however, we must be careful that the desire doesn't consume us and
lead us into debt. We are living in a "fad" society. Products are

designed to interest you temporarily until the next fad comes through. There is a novelty about being a trend-setter and owning the latest fashion. In school, kids always want to have the newest shoes *first*, and their parents are willing to spend $100 to $200 for one pair of shoes. Within six months, the style changes and those shoes become outdated.

When people make purchases to make them feel better about themselves, they have fallen into the debt trap. *Money that is spent on high fashion can't restore low self-esteem.* Remember that your life is not made up of the material things that you possess (see Lk. 12:15), but of the relationship that you have with God. When that is in proper order, all other needs and desires will be met (see Mt. 6:33).

In the Book of Galatians, Paul was dealing with the fact that the Galatians were gullible and attracted to new and curious things, so much so that it caused them to stray away from the truth (see Gal. 1:6-10; 3:1). Every day people stray away from what they *know* they need to do concerning their finances because of their desire and curiosity for new things. Just as this problem brought in false brethren to the Galatians (see Gal. 2:4), so an overwhelming desire for new things will open you up to debt's relentless attack.

Keep in mind that bargains seldom come with a brand-name attached to them, and that hot brand-names are like the heavens and earth—destined to pass away.

Lack of Discipline

Proverbs 25:28 says, "He that hath no rule over his own spirit is like a city that is broken down, and without walls." Discipline is the key to success in all areas of life. When you feed your flesh more than you feed your spirit, your flesh has more control. As a result, you can't tell your flesh to "shut up" and let your spirit take control. Your flesh has the most power. It must be disciplined to come under the submission of your spirit through prayer, fasting, and study of the Word.

When your flesh is not disciplined in your finances, you will find yourself saying, "I know I can't afford this, but...," or "I don't know where the money is going to come from to pay for this!" If you don't know where the money is going to come from to cover that check or to pay the credit card bill, it is *insane* for you to make the purchase! Your faith is not designed to compensate for your lack of order and discipline. *Every time you go to the mall, watch seductive TV ads, or read magazine ads, you are breaking down your discipline and your ability to resist temptation* (see Ps. 101:3).

The fruit of discipline is goals. Goals help to keep you from getting caught in debt by giving purpose to your spending and discipline in your finances. The reason so many people get caught in the trap of overspending is because they have no vision. That, in turn, causes them to cast off restraint, especially in the area of finances (see Prov. 29:18 TLB). When you line up your spending with your vision, structure it with your goals, and base it on your purpose, debt doesn't stand a chance.

Immediate Gratification

In spending, you should always buy what you need before you buy what you want. This is called "Priority Spending/ Purchasing." As a believer, your first financial responsibility is to *pay your tithe and offering* unto the Lord (see Prov. 3:9-10; Mal. 3:8-10). After that, the Bible is clear that you should *pay your bills and debts* (see Ps. 37:21; Prov. 3:27-28), and then *save* money (see Prov. 21:20 TLB). Finally, you can then purchase your wants and desires (see Ps. 37:4).

Debt tempts people the same way that sex tempts singles. It is God's will for people to have sex, just as it is God's will for people to have nice things. However, there is a time and a season for those things (see Eccles. 3:1). *Just as sex is reserved for marriage, pleasure spending is reserved for those who are current on their bills and are relentlessly attacking debt.*

The devil tempts us to go into debt by giving us an opportunity that we can't pass up (e.g., a clearance sale), and if we're not careful, we fall right into sin. Just as a man may ask a woman (or vice versa), "Why wait? You can have it now," debt asks the same questions, and we accept its offers.

The same ways that singles use to prevent fornication can be used to prevent debt accumulation. Keep yourself out of compromising positions (e.g., malls and shopping with credit cards) and see the reward in waiting (the ability to pay cash for the item and not having to go into debt for it). Sometimes having it now can prove to be disastrous. Though we live in a "right now" society, *God knows that the process of saving for an item will help to mature us to handle it and give us a greater appreciation.*

God forced the Israelites to take the longer route to get to the Promised Land because they were not prepared for the battle that came with the short-cut (see Ex. 13:17-18). Likewise, God knows that you are not mature enough to handle the responsibility that comes from making certain purchases right now. Although you have the option to go the short way, *God is leading you the longer way* so that you can be developed. The battle that you would have encountered in the shorter way would most likely have overtaken you and brought destruction to your finances. ***Always remember that the process must come before the product.***

Trying to Impress Others

Many times people spend money that they don't have on things they don't need to impress people who don't matter. Trying to keep up with the Joneses will always leave your finances looking tired. It is your lifestyle, not your material possessions, that determine your level of blessing. Many people want to give the *appearance* of being blessed without having the foundation of blessing. Consequently, they find themselves living a lie and never being satisfied (see Prov. 27:20).

Just because God has blessed someone with a million dollars, a nice car, or a husband, doesn't mean that we're entitled to the same blessing. God blesses us according to our purpose and our needs (see Prov. 30:8-9; Phil. 4:19). God will give us the desires of our hearts only if those desires aren't contrary to His heart.

Most people who are in uncontrollable debt don't understand how their purpose is affected by their finances. Therefore, they try to acquire things that *people*, not God, willed for them to have. When this is the case, God is under no obligation to help you pay for what He hasn't authorized. God has a season for you to buy, but your season of saving always precedes your season of spending. When you make a purchase out of season, you get what you wanted (the item purchased), but you lose what you had (e.g., relationship with God, peace, contentment)—all because you tried to impress someone else.

Trying to Overcome Depression

There are people reading this book right now who have tried to use shopping as a means of alleviating depression. Rather than deal with the root of the issue, people go and buy themselves new items, which provides them with an immediate temporary high. Buying provides a temporary high with a long-term low. The reality of the bill overtakes the superficial high of the purchase and adds to the previous state of depression. *You must understand that the traveling companion of debt is depression.*

The root of your depression must be exposed so that it can be dealt with. Covering the root instead of attacking it will perpetuate it and cause it to become uncontrollable. Learning from your previous mistakes will help you to avoid constant torment. If the last state of depression that you were in was based on finances, give earnest heed to that and avoid repeating the things that led to your depression.

Jesus never felt depression. He also was a perfect steward and money manager. He always had money for taxes (see Mt. 17:24-27), and He provided for His disciples. Any person who could feed 12 men for three and a half years had to have been able to budget. If your depression stems from your financial condition, then it is insane to get into debt in an attempt to overcome it. Don't allow the enemy to fake you out with gratifying your flesh. Attack your depression with spiritual consistency (prayer, fasting, study of the Word, and fellowship) and discipline in natural things (saving, investing, budgeting, exercise, etc.).

Attempting to Fill Voids in Your Life

Every person has a "vacuum" in his or her spirit that God created and that only He can fill. When we attempt to fill that void with other things, we will never be satisfied. *Total sufficiency and happiness come from relationship with God.* Consider the rich young ruler in Luke 18:18-23. He had money and power, but he knew that there was something missing in his life. Until he followed and made covenant with Jesus, he was not going to be happy.

Many people today are like that young man. They have material wealth, cars, clothes, and the fawning of the opposite sex. But they still aren't totally satisfied. There was a well-known actor interviewed on *20/20* who had been afflicted with a life-threatening disease that took his ability to speak and much of his physical strength. This man has millions of dollars, a loving wife, committed friends, and adoring fans. However, he was raised an atheist. As this disease began to take over his body, he made the statement to his friends that he wished he believed in God. He came to the realization that his material possessions and worldly success could not take God's place in his life.

Money never has been and never will be the solution to every problem. Increases in income and spending are never compensation for knowing God in a personal way. Buying things to fill God's purpose is idolatry. Whenever you don't allow Christ to rule your life, you will constantly look for other things to fill that void!

We must allow the simplicity of life to bring contentment (see Phil. 4:12). People often mention the things that they don't have as the reason they're not happy. People who are content in Christ, their marriage, and their purpose usually don't overspend, because they are full of life (see Jn. 14:6). Whatever we allow to fill us will be the deciding factor of our happiness and joy. *Remember, people spend money in an attempt to fill a void that has been left by God!*

Debt Starts Off as Fun

People's lives are motivated by having fun. The thought of relaxing on Saturday and Sunday gives many people the motivation to work Monday through Friday. Similarly, debt offers itself as a way for many to do the things that they want to do. The drawback is that you always pay for more than what you get by going into debt. *Debt raises the cost of your fun in an attempt to eventually rob you of it.* Sure, a family vacation is exciting and refreshing. But when a couple realizes the amount of money they've spent on the trip, the fun turns to worry as they attempt to slow their spending.

Debt never plays fair. There is always an element of deception in it. It is imperative that we discern debt's true intention and use it for our advantage. (See Chapter 9, "The Possibilities of Debt.") Too often we focus on how things start off without "understanding its end" (see Ps. 73:17). When we misplace our focus, we provide ourselves with immediate gratification without considering the long-term impact of our decisions. *Debt is one of the few ways that allows pleasure to come before the process.*

In every instance in the Bible where God made a promise (pleasure), He took the people through a process. (See Exodus 13:17-22 on the Israelites and Genesis 37–41 on Joseph.) The question that you must ask yourself is, "Would I be able to live this lifestyle without a credit card or loan?" If the answer is "no," then you cannot afford the purchases you are making. Debt is your provider, not God, which is a form of idolatry.

Low Self-Esteem

Many times when people have low self-esteem, they try to become something that they're not. People get into debt trying to look, dress, or act like someone else in the hopes that being identified with that person will increase their worth in other people's eyes and eventually increase their self-esteem.

Paul said in Galatians 1:10, "For do I now persuade men, or God? *or do I seek to please men? for if I yet pleased men, I should not be the servant of Christ.*" Many of the Galatian church members were turning away. As a spokesman for the gospel, Paul could make such a bold statement because he knew who he was in Christ and understood that his value was fixed. Therefore, he let the people know that he wasn't looking to please man.

Many people today are caught in debt trying to please a person instead of being pleasing to the Father. Consequently, they "pay the price" to be accepted by their peers without counting the cost. *Looking at things to determine your worth will never give you an accurate reading.* Things are never a valid admittance ticket to success. They give you a false sense of well-being and never deal with the problem. The best cure for low self-esteem is a relationship with Christ. He's the only One who can fill any void in your life. (See "Trying to Overcome Depression" earlier in this chapter.)

New things are short-term and their effects soon wear off. *Although the thrill of fashion disappears, the effects of debt will continue to linger.*

No Emergency Plan

When there is no emergency plan, everything becomes an emergency. Many people back themselves into a corner by not preparing for possible expenses. When an unexpected expense occurs, the only option that they have is a credit card or a loan. Emergencies attract debt because it gives people a reason to borrow. Proverbs 22:3 (TLB) says, "A prudent man foresees the difficulties ahead and prepares for them; the simpleton goes blindly on and suffers the consequences."

A sign of wisdom is planning. Though you don't know *exactly* what will happen, you do know that *something* will happen that will require extra money (e.g., church obligation, car trouble, illness). By planning, you are prepared to handle both potential emergencies and opportunities. Many times people get better prices on homes, cars, and land because they are in a position to buy on the spot.

Loan and finance companies are in business because of people's lack of preparation. They are successful in convincing people that they can't and shouldn't pay for unexpected expenses. By being convinced that our credit card, finance company, church, or friends should be our emergency fund, we don't establish one of our own. ***Whenever you ask someone for something before you ask God, it's idolatry.***

If you are a parent, how would you feel if your child always went to another child's parents or to another couple for all his needs before consulting you? The pain you would feel is the same way God feels. It is an insult to Him when we can't trust Him for our needs. He knows what we need even before we ask (see Mt. 6:8).

Though He told us to "take no thought for your life" (Mt. 6:25), that doesn't negate the importance of planning. The best way to handle an emergency is to cut expenses, but many times we look for ways to make more money. Very rarely is making more money the solution; it's in the proper handling of what you make. *Although it takes adjustments to handle emergencies, anything that is unprepared for will always be unexpected.*

Lack of Planning

There are some instances when the situation is not an emergency but an opportunity or a desire. God wants to give you the desires of your heart (see Ps. 37:4), but planning is necessary in this area as well. When making a purchase, it is wise to count the cost (see Lk. 14:28), to see how it will affect your budget, and to save for it for a season. By looking down the road, you can in some ways predict what will happen and be prepared to deal with the resulting situations.

Many times we make spiritual excuses for our procrastination and poor planning by saying that God will work it out somehow. Then when things don't go the way we thought, we are forced to go into debt. *Being busy living for today will cause you to forget about tomorrow.* Realize that there is at least one tomorrow for every today. Although it is not promised, it should be prepared for. *Why should God give you a tomorrow if you have no idea what you're going to do with it?* If you don't know the purpose of your next day, you're bound to abuse it.

By looking at some of the most common things that we don't plan for, we see that none of them come as a surprise. For example, Christmas comes every year at the same time, but there are countless numbers of families who wait until the last minute to go Christmas shopping, usually because they wait until the last minute to set aside money. When there is not enough money to purchase gifts and pay bills, we are forced to charge. Therefore, on Christmas morning, no one is disappointed—except Jesus, because we failed to buy Him a gift (e.g., a special offering to His Church; help for someone less fortunate; etc. [see Prov. 19:17 TLB].)

Every family wants and deserves a vacation. Everything about a vacation is determined by you, including the time you take it and the price you pay. But, because of poor planning, many families get into debt and turn a controllable situation into an uncontrollable one.

Your children will go back to school every year, needing school clothes, and eventually will go off to college. Your church's annual events include a year-end pledge, a pastoral anniversary, or a special building fund. Your car will definitely need some service this year and your family will have birthdays. All these things are expected and can be easily prepared for. The key is to stop living for today only and to consider the impact that today's actions will have on your life tomorrow.

Believing That You Deserve More Than You Presently Have

In Matthew 25:14-30, Jesus tells the parable of the talents. Notice that the master gave goods to each servant according to their ability to handle them. *You can tell what God trusts you with based on what you have.* The attitude of the world is that hard work qualifies you for a shopping spree and that because you have earned the money, you are entitled to buy whatever you want. However, people work harder at *making* money than they do at *managing* money. They want the reward of their labor without assuming the responsibility.

It is by the grace of God that we don't get what we deserve, both good and bad. In the story of the prodigal son, the young man wanted what he deserved, for he was heir to an inheritance. Though he deserved it, he was not ready to handle it, and it eventually turned into his downfall. Though we are Christians and want to represent Christ well, it is a bad testimony to attempt to look good by getting into debt. *Debt is the quickest way to get what you want, but it is usually not the best way.* Accruing interest, finance charges, and possible late fees usually raise a sale price far beyond the regular price, after counting all costs.

Many people feel that they only live once, and since they never had anything growing up and they're Christians now, they think God wants them to have the best. Their thinking is, "If the world has it, surely I as a Christian should too." (See Psalm 73; Proverbs 23:17-18.) These are all good motivations for properly planning to acquire what you desire, but they are not reasons to get into debt. Everything has a season (see Eccles. 3:1), and your season of *spending* is always preceded by your season of *saving*.

Poor Money Management Training From Their Parents

Whatever children see their parents doing in managing finances leaves an impression on them and usually determines their own financial habits. Proverbs 22:6 says that we are to "train up a child in the way he should go: and when he is old, he will not depart from it." If they enjoyed a lifestyle that was afforded them by debt, then they are inclined to use the same method in acquiring the same lifestyle.

Parents influence this pattern of behavior by co-signing for their child's first car, obtaining whole life insurance policies so that their children can *borrow* the money later in life (which perpetuates debt), giving them credit cards before they even have a job, fighting over money, and lying to creditors. Most parents can't tell their children that if they follow their instructions, the children will live a long life (see Prov. 4:1-4). We can only pass down what we have. It will take discipline and prayer to break the current cycle in families today.

Wrong Priorities

Too many people believe that what we have shows the world who we are. The appearance of prosperity makes many think that a person has more of God in his life. Our employer may think that we are successful, making us worth more to the company. Our friends assume that we're doing something right to have the things that we have. We even boost ourselves up, thinking that we've arrived.

However, many people sacrifice time with God, their spouse, and their children for the sake of acquiring things (e.g., working long hours, constantly in ministry). Proper spending priorities will make your money more efficient. Remember that *first things first, lifts the spending curse.* Your first responsibility as a Christian is to pay tithes and give an offering. Secondly, you are responsible for your bills and necessary living expenses (food, basic clothes, phone, shelter). After this, you should save money (see Prov. 21:20 TLB). Finally, you can buy things that you desire that are within your budget.

Restructuring your spending priorities is vital to the resurrection of your finances. All money that you spend is an investment. Therefore, only invest in things that will yield the greatest return and let your assets outweigh your liabilities.

Chapter 7

The Power of Debt: Why It Is So Hard to Break Free From Debt

In all our experience, we have never met a person who enjoyed being in debt. Obviously people enjoy what debt can initially produce, but when the subsequent responsibility kicks in, debt loses its pleasure and manifests its true identity. Many people have been motivated to attempt to get out of debt; however, when their attempt failed, the first question they asked is, "Why?" Here we will examine some of the key reasons it's so hard to break free from the power of debt.

Debt Enhances Your Social Status

Everyone wants to have a sense of status and importance, especially in his or her circle of relationships. For many people, debt is the only way in which they can look important and get the attention that they desire. *It is impossible to enjoy the lifestyle of success as a financial failure.* **What you have will never determine who you are, and insecurity is a breeding ground for debt.**

People idolize debt, relying on it to get things that they feel they never would have gotten any other way. Credit cards are a means of getting jewelry, clothes, yard equipment, and even cash, that people can't afford. Many people take out consumer or home equity loans to purchase unnecessary items without realizing that the product is not officially theirs until they pay off their debt. When you purchase an item with someone else's money, you are merely borrowing the merchandise until the day that you pay off the debt.

With debt, you obtain things before your season. However, when you do that, you are getting a harvest that is not yet ripe. Picking fruit out of season will increase your risk of getting fruit that's not ripe. You also cast an illusion of success, which is nothing but witchcraft in your finances. You manipulate and alter your appearance to disguise your true identity. This constitutes living a lie and God cannot bless you until you become honest with yourself.

When you get hooked on a lifestyle that your paycheck alone can't support, you never become satisfied and, consequently, will never have enough. Debt allows you to live a lifestyle far beyond what you make. It's like having a "sugar daddy" who provides for all your needs, but you must constantly pay the price, even after the relationship is over. The key to escaping this type of bondage is to derive your identity and importance from Christ and not allow the world to program your mind into thinking that your material items determine your status (see Lk. 12:15).

Debt Only Requires You to Pay the Minimum Payment

When you receive your credit card or loan statement, it tells you what your balance is and then gives you the "payment due." *This is actually the minimum payment due.* For credit cards, it is usually 2 percent of your total balance, or about $15, whichever is greater. For loans, it is the amount that will stretch the term to its fullest length. If your credit card balance is $1,000, the company requires you to *pay* only 2 percent, or $20, while the company charges you between 15 and 22 percent interest.

If that balance were $3,000 at an interest rate of 19.8 percent, and assuming that you made no new purchases, it would take you 39 years to pay off your balance if you just paid the minimum payment. You also would have paid over $10,000 in non-deductible interest. Though the payments are small, the length of the balance affects the big picture. Wisdom considers the long-term effects of a lingering balance and makes proper adjustments (see Prov. 22:3).

What is amazing is that if people had to pay more of their out-standing balance, they would, but there's no sense of urgency. The attitude is, if the people you owe are not pressed for payment, then they shouldn't press you to pay. People are defeated by bills because they are always on the defense and never take the offense. A football team might have a great defense and hold their opponent to three points, but if they never mount an effective scoring drive on their offense, they will still lose the game.

To avoid financial hardship is not a cause for celebration but a chance to capitalize. It is imperative that we see the long-term advantage to paying more than the minimum on our debts. Though a minimum payment is small, it gives the loan its longest life span and takes more of your life (money). This small payment is a vital organ to the well-being of debt. If it is destroyed by always paying greatly above the minimum, debt's power will be weakened.

Debt Is Accepted as Normal in Society

In biblical times, unpaid debt was not tolerated. Rather, it was punished by forcible acquisition of your property, torment, or slavery of you and/or your family (see 2 Kings 4:1-7; Neh. 5:1-5; Mt. 18:25-34). In today's society, debt is accepted as normal and is even expected in everyone's life. However, the same punishments that were given to those with unpaid debt in biblical times are given today.

Debt is slavery (see Prov. 22:7), and the greater the debt you owe, the more enslaved you become. Forcible acquisition of your property includes repossession and auctions of your assets. Torment begins in the mind through worry and stress and eventually manifests itself in the physical realm through headaches, ulcers, fatigue, and possible nervous breakdowns. Television promotion associates debt with success when companies use celebrities to advertise their credit cards and financial programs.

Credit cards and quick loan approvals are viewed as a reward for being successful and a sign that somebody "trusts" you enough to loan you money. A credit card helps to establish your credit and it is viewed as a negative many times if you don't have one or if you pay it off each month. Many companies will request the return of your credit card because they don't make a profit on you.

Debt attempts to provide you with everything you need to function. Your credit card is used as identification, can secure a hotel reservation, airline ticket, or car rental, and acts as an agent for you, conducting business when you are not there. Your credit card number has the same power and authority as your word. It proves itself to be a sufficient replacement for cash, is accepted in more places than your personal check, and gives you access to purchasing and negotiating power with a swipe, phone call, or light paperwork.

Debt will even reward you for timely payment with upgraded cards, higher credit limits, cash back, deferment of payment, or free gifts. Yet, in spite of the attractive packaging and bells and whistles, debt is still a killer and can't be trusted.

Interest Rates and Fees

Debt feeds off interest; it is what gives debt life. Do you remember the example in which it takes 39 years to pay off a credit card balance of $3,000 with a 19.8 percent interest rate by paying just the minimum payment? If the interest rate dropped to 18 percent, all other things remaining constant, it would still take *31 years* to pay off the balance just paying the minimum payment. The power of interest is that 1.8 percent interest equals *8 years of additional payment*!

Companies also use over-the-limit fees, cash advance fees, and late fees to keep you in debt. Over-the-limit fees can cost you hundreds of dollars, in addition to your charges and interest. Consequently, a person could pay hundreds of dollars on their credit card and still not be paying on the balance of their purchases. You are paying for something and getting nothing in return.

The power of interest rates is key to the power of debt. *Anybody* can get *somebody* to give him or her a loan, if the terms are right! People with poor credit pay higher interest rates for credit cards and all loans. *A poor credit past will always mean a more expensive credit future.*

Higher interest rates are due to the greater risk that is incurred in giving credit and loaning money to someone with poor credit. Additionally, because credit cards are unsecured, the default rate is very high; thus, everyone pays a higher rate.

When you pay only the minimum (which most people do), the majority of your payment goes to interest, and not to the outstanding balance. Credit card issuers earn about 75 percent of their revenues from people who don't pay in full each month. Studies show that on average, credit cards are twice as profitable as all other banking activities. Because of this, lenders hate customers who pay off their debt monthly. Some banks charge no-interest fees (meaning, if you haven't accrued any interest, they will charge you a standard fee), while others have actually canceled the customer's card and closed his credit account.

Just think, when you are a good steward, the banks take back their cards because they make no profit from you, while people who run up stupid debt are given higher limits! Banks personify debt's personality.

These days, what used to disqualify you for credit approval now makes you a worthwhile risk. Now that bankruptcy is higher than it ever has been, credit card companies and lending institutions seek people with bankruptcy records, whereas in the past, bankruptcy would almost automatically disqualify a person from credit or a loan. Why? Banks can charge a person who has filed bankruptcy higher interest rates; laws prohibit those people from refiling bankruptcy within a certain period; and all their old debts have been canceled, leaving them with more money to pay for their new debts.

Pride

Pride keeps the financially crippled in a wheelchair. Debt has given people a way of life that they know they can't afford but are unwilling to give up. People refuse to lower and change their lifestyle to accommodate their need to improve their financial situation. Only greed wants you to look successful before you are successful.

When people are forced to change their lifestyle, they become self-conscious, thinking that people will assume that they are failures and not as successful as they thought. In actuality, that is the truth. You weren't as successful as they thought if your success was determined by material things that you had but couldn't afford. People who live like that are living a lie and playing right into the court of debt.

Debt is deceptive and it will cause you to be deceptive for the sake of your reputation. To go and seek help will mean admitting that you have a problem; and until you face the problem, it can't be fixed. The reason a mirror doesn't lie is because it merely casts a reflection. People who have a false sense of identity refuse to look in a mirror for fear it will reveal the true them. Confession is the mirror that reveals the true state of your finances.

With every person, church, business, etc., that we have dealt with, none of them could fix their problem until they first confessed that they had one. After confessing the fact that there *is* a problem, they must confess what the real problem is and take full responsibility. Many times people blame their bosses for their financial difficulty, saying that they don't make enough. Although that is possible, it's also rare. The truth is that many people are terrible at managing what they make. The good news is that God *can* and *will* take what you have to create what you need!

Release the pride in your life and confess your problems. Then God can move in your finances and begin to bring deliverance from debt and poverty, and move you into true prosperity.

Debt Releases a Spirit of Depression

In order to defeat debt, you must be motivated. Debt depresses you when you find yourself constantly making payments and yet the balance isn't significantly reduced. Also, because it appears that credit card bills and loan payments all come at the same time, you feel overwhelmed by them. This robs you of your will and destroys your sense of urgency.

Debt's goal is to get you to stop fighting and surrender to its will. Debt and depression are traveling companions; you don't have one without the other. Depression takes your vision and gives you a sense of hopelessness. When your vision is gone, you will soon perish (cast off restraint), which is a sign that you don't care anymore (see Prov. 29:18). At that point, your defeat is inevitable. Debt has a systematic plan to destroy you, but God has a plan that will deliver you from debt and defeat depression in your life.

Debt Is Easily Accessible, Regardless of Your Credit Record

Debt is ruthless in nature; it doesn't care about the age of its victims. If you are 18 and can sign your name (even though you don't have a job), you are a legitimate candidate for credit. By placing people in bondage at an early age, companies ensure a long-term relationship that will guarantee them future revenue.

Even in your own home, you can be in debt in less than 24 hours by using the telephone and getting approval.

As stated in previous chapters, companies pass on names of potential card owners to other companies in an attempt to take advantage of a person's poor spending habits. Even your children's names could get on a mailing list to be preapproved for a credit card. Many people like to use multiple cards, and will even use their child's card, which plays right into the debt trap.

As we said in the previous section, companies are now targeting people with bankruptcies or poor credit records because the companies can charge higher interest rates. These businesses play on the desire of these people with poor credit to have a credit card. When these people receive a card, it gives them a sense of importance and progress, when in actuality they have just signed away their lives and future earning potential.

So many people have fed into debt that it has reproduced itself into different types. Demand for credit cards is so high that department stores, gas stations, jewelry stores, and novelty shops have specific cards for their stores. Banks have created check cards, combining the convenience of a credit card with access to your checking account. By doing this, people continue to spend more than they would with cash, and the money is immediately deducted from their checking account, removing any grace period. All this is competition for your dollar, and *each company is using convenience as its primary weapon.*

When loan and finance companies see you paying debts on time, they will "do you a favor" and loan you more money without increasing your monthly payment. Now you become free advertisement for them by telling all the saints how God blessed you and that He'll do the same for them. Just as the new Egyptian king put the Israelites in bondage (see Ex. 1:8-14), debt puts you in bondage as you acquire more of it.

Notice that today everyone has a way for a person to get credit. Companies are constantly developing new ways to get you into debt, and it's working. Companies will loan up to 125 percent of the value of your home (minus your first mortgage), whereas in the past, you could get only between 50 and 80 percent of your home's value for a loan. Although it is treated like an unsecured loan (the rates are higher than a regular loan), the house becomes security, and if payment is not made, the house is lost.

For example, if you purchased a $200,000 house with a 10 percent down payment, you would pay $20,000 up front, making your first mortgage $180,000. At 125 percent, the value of the house is $250,000. By subtracting $180,000 (the value of your first mortgage) from $250,000, you get the amount that you're eligible for, which in this case is $70,000. This means that you must stay enslaved to that house longer because you owe $70,000 more than the house costs and may be worth!

The companies say that an added benefit is that the interest *may be* tax deductible and the payment will be lower than a regular loan. They forget to tell you that the reason it is low is because the loan is for 15 to 25 years. *You should never get caught in the trap of keeping a mortgage on your house for a tax deduction!* There are limits to your deduction and the overall cost is not worth it: The IRS will not permit you to deduct interest on loan amounts exceeding the fair market value of the house; interest rates are higher than that of a regular home loan; and the risk of losing your home increases. Debt has found another way to enslave you.

People Like the Feeling That Comes From a New Purchase

Spending can and many times does become an addiction. Purchasing something new gives people a high and *temporarily* delivers them from their problems. Their focus shifts from their current situation to the new addition to their wardrobe, garage, or living room. It is a false sense of satisfaction and a lapse from reality.

For many people, spending can be therapeutic, relieving them from stress and pressures. However, people fail to realize that today's spending will be the cause for tomorrow's pressures. *It is important to realize that spending turns into debt and that the therapy you used to relieve stress and pressure eventually turns into the cause.*

Nothing is wrong with buying new things, but they must be bought at the right time and in moderation. Just like prescription drugs, if spending is done outside of the "recommended dosage," it can become harmful. Although the world says that what feels good can't be wrong or bad, the Word (see Prov. 21:17) and common sense tells us that's not true. The goal in taking drugs is to get high. Though the high gives you an initial rush, its destruction is far greater than its benefits. And just as drugs look to destroy your body, spending will turn evil in an effort to destroy your finances.

Though some debt is incurred through accidents and emergencies, the leading cause is overspending. Most people spend money trying to fill a void that only God can fill. People look for happiness, fulfillment, self-esteem, and identity in their spending and material possessions. All these are things that we find in a personal relationship with Christ. It is only there that your joy, happiness, and fulfillment can become permanent.

The Plan Required to Get Out of Debt Is Too Complicated

Debt often intimidates us because it seems too hard to get out of. So many of their friends have failed in defeating debt that people refuse to try. It takes time and patience to develop a plan to get out. Some people have a problem with leisure spending, while others need to cut their expenses. The key is knowing what works for you.

Remember the story of David and Goliath, where Saul gave David his helmet of brass and his coat of mail (see 1 Sam. 17:38-39)? David said that he couldn't use them because he wasn't used to them, though they were part of the traditional style of fighting. In order to defeat debt, you must know what method of attack to use and when to try something different. If someone in debt gets a second job, but they remain in debt, that tactic is not working. They need to try another one.

The problem is that most people know of only one way to get out of debt, and that is to get a second job. When that way fails, they become too lazy to develop an effective plan and fail in their attempt. Proverbs 13:4 says, "The soul of the sluggard desireth, and hath nothing: but the soul of the diligent shall be made fat."

Now spiritual excuses come into play. We begin waiting on our miracle, whether it be a huge blessing or a miraculous debt cancellation, without working toward the goal. *Most people see the big picture but refuse to develop the blueprints.* Though you went into debt quickly, it takes far more time and effort to get out. Eventually, you get impatient and give up all hope. This is debt's plan to destroy your will and keep you in bondage. (Get ready, for in the next chapter we are going to give you a plan that is guaranteed to defeat debt.)

People Don't Like Being Without Money

Studies show that people spend 35 percent more with a credit card than they do with cash. Why? They don't feel the initial outflow of cash. Money in your pocket or wallet makes you feel successful, powerful, and important. Being without money frustrates most people, whether they're debt-free or not. Which scenario is more appealing to you: to owe $3,000 and have $3,000 in the bank, or to owe no money and have none in the bank? If you chose the first one, you're probably in debt now.

When people get their tax refund check or a large sum of money, why do they spend it or hold it instead of paying off a debt? (In Second Kings 4:7, when the woman obtained money, she paid her debts.) Part of the reason some people hold on to it is because they aren't used to having money, and whenever they get some they want to savor the moment. People who have money know how to handle it. Part of handling it is paying off bills and outstanding debts.

Debt preys on people who are not accustomed to having money or things. It gets you to charge your purchase instead of spending your cash, or to spend your last dollar in an effort to keep you in bondage forever.

Payment Deferrals and Balance Transfers

Credit card companies are not stupid. They know when you're going to need cash the most. That's why during the holidays and peak vacation times companies begin to offer ways for you to skip payment for the next couple of months. However, most people fail to understand that while they are making no payments on *new* purchases, their *old* purchases are still accruing interest. *Therefore, they are paying interest on the purchase and interest on the interest.*

Credit card and loan companies are constantly coming up with new ways to make your life "easier," while they profit greatly from your ignorance. They will grant lower interest rates to get you to transfer all your debts to one card. When you do this, it frees up your other credit cards and allows you to charge them up to the limit again. Some offer low introductory interest rates, causing you to feel the liberty to spend more, but those low rates are for a *season*. Then the rate goes up to its normal 15 to 22 percent.

Cash advances are another way that card companies get you swamped in debt. They play on the convenience that they will loan you cash without a loan application and will even waive the cash advance fees. What they fail to tell you is that the interest rate is usually *more* for a cash advance than for a charge. Even your friends will encourage you to "card-hop." When one introductory rate goes up, move to another card. Credit cards are like bombs, though, delicate and dangerous. Unless they are handled by a person who understands them and can use them to his advantage, they will cause destruction to his finances.

Companies Offer Either No-Term
or Long-Term Payment Options

Some companies don't give you a time limit to pay off the card. They just give you a line of credit that you have access to for life, thus taking off the pressure to pay monthly (e.g., credit cards). The goal is to keep you in debt for the rest of your life so that the company can continue to make residual income from your purchases. Employees of these companies can keep their jobs and possibly make large bonuses off your spending habits.

With larger purchases such as a house, a car, or a business, loan amounts are usually higher, so companies increase the term of the loan so they can lower the payment. The problem is that a longer term extends your time in slavery. *People are more concerned with payments than they are with price.* Though the price may be high, if the payments are low, then people are more inclined to pay more. When a person has lower payments, they have more money to spend on other things without considering that there is another payment due the following month.

Many times people fail to realize that longer term loans have higher interest rates, meaning that more interest is paid. There is more time for you to become conditioned to debt, and you become like the lame man in John 5, who accepted his condition as a part of life. As you pay down your loan, the lender will entice you with more money without changing your payment, starting the cycle all over again.

Credit Cards Are Accepted By All Types of Vendors

In the past, credit card debt was difficult to get into because few vendors accepted them. Now, everyone accepts them. The sudden shift is due to the extra spending that is done with a credit card versus cash because people don't feel the initial outflow. Vendors also know that credit cards expand people's buying power where they can spend money they don't have, therefore increasing the vendor's chance of making a sale.

Everybody says that we should use our credit cards. Grocery stores and gas stations have installed machines for you to pay for your purchases with your credit card. Some airlines offer discounts to people who pay with a credit card. Tax preparers, clothing stores, restaurants (fast food), and even funeral homes advertise their willingness to take credit cards. Because of the widespread availability and convenience, credit cards are the hottest way to spend. All the while, debt lurks in the shadows, looking to pounce on every victim of this fad.

Though debt has the appearance of making your life look easier by giving you one bill, eliminating check writing, tracking possible tax deductions, and allowing you to use someone else's money, it strips you of your financial freedom and forces you into a life of limitation and bondage.

In Exodus chapter 1, the children of Israel had a life of "convenience" because their meals and housing were provided by their masters. They were, however, slaves in that nothing belonged to them and they were subject to someone else. Debt operates the same way by offering the convenience of money and enabling you to appear to possess things, but in reality you own nothing; they belong to the lender/slave master (see Prov. 22:7). As the Israelites became impatient in the wilderness because they couldn't see their way out, they talked of going back to Egypt. In the same way, when attacking debt appears to be an insurmountable task, you begin to think of giving up. But as Paul said, be willing to "press toward the mark for the prize of the high calling of God in Christ Jesus" (Phil. 3:14), which in the case of your finances is to be debt-free.

Chapter 8

The Plan: Defeating Debt Forever

The purpose of this chapter is to help you develop a comprehensive plan to defeat debt. In the previous seven chapters, we gave you an extensive analysis of debt's personality, power, characteristics, plan of attack, purpose, and process. In the Word of God, Jesus left us instructions on how to defeat satan, and here we are giving you His plan on how to defeat debt.

Before going to war, you must decide if you are willing to pay the price to get the victory. In war there are casualties, expenses, and sacrifices. If you are going to defeat debt, then you must be willing to die to your will, invest in learning how to get out and stay out of debt (for example, the purchase of this book), and sacrifice some of the luxuries that got you into debt. Deuteronomy 15:6 gives us the promise that we will lend and not borrow; therefore, we must be willing to go through the process of obtaining the promise. These are things that you *must* do if you want to even stand a chance against debt. Just as the devil has deceived us about sin's consequences, so debt has deceived us of its consequences.

But remember, if God knows that you're going to fight debt, He'll always provide a weapon!

1. You Must Face It Before You Can Fix It

No drug addict or alcoholic can possibly overcome his condition before admitting that he has a problem, and then facing it. David never denied the size of Goliath, nor the fact that he was incapable of defeating him by human ability. He never made an excuse as to why he couldn't challenge him; he knew that the Lord was on his side. If we know that the Lord is on our side, then there should be no problem in facing debt.

All the other soldiers had skill, experience, and resources. Even with all those, if the enemy is not faced, it cannot be defeated. We have met people who are literally afraid to open their bills because they didn't want to face the reality of their financial condition (which is called financial denial). However, the condition remains.

Often times Christians use religious excuses to cover up their irresponsibility. For example, a debt-infested Christian may say that it is God's season of suffering for him before He brings him into prosperity. But this person has no budget, no savings account, and has missed paying tithes and offerings. Proverbs 19:3 (TLB) says, "A man may ruin his chances by his own foolishness and then blame it on the Lord!" *God can't be blamed for your financial failure when you refuse to obey His Word concerning finances.*

People continue to make poor financial decisions because negative consequences are not immediate. Wisdom is seeing your problem from a distance and making provisions early (see Prov. 22:3). How do you face your problems? Go to Appendix A and list *every bill* that you have, in order from smallest to largest. This is your first step in destroying your enemy called debt.

2. See Debt As a *Hostile* Enemy to the Will of God

This entire book has been devoted to revealing debt for what it really is, instead of the "blessing" that so many people make it out to be. *Debt is the natural enemy of healthy finances, and until you realize it, you will never fight it with the conviction and passion that it takes to defeat it.* Debt is a *hostile* enemy; that means it is not just opposed to your advancement in the will of God, but is an opponent that wars against and antagonizes you with the sole purpose of destroying your finances.

Debt is set against the idea that you can be debt-free and against the calling and conviction that you have about prosperity. *It isn't set against **your** will, but the **will of God** in your life.* Debt knows that your will is tainted by sin and that it takes the will of God to regenerate your thinking and desires to fulfill your purpose. Therefore, *debt sets your will against God's will by providing an unscriptural way for you to get the things that you want.*

Throughout this book we have shown that God hates perpetual debt and debt that was incurred by abusive spending. The will of God completed in your life guarantees the destruction of debt. The perfect will of God is that we be conformed to the image of Jesus. One of Jesus' characteristics was being totally debt-free, so much so that He could pay your debt. The devil had *nothing* in Jesus (see Jn. 14:30), and that included His finances. Because of this, Jesus could walk in the perfect will of God in every area of life.

Debt is an enemy because it wants the opposite of what God wants for you. God desires for you to be able to lend (see Deut. 15:6), be prosperous (see Ps. 37:4; 3 Jn. 2), be blessed to help others (see Gen. 12:3), have peace (see Jn. 14:27), and live in abundance (see Jn. 10:10). Debt wants to keep you out of these promises and out of your inheritance.

God's will has two parts: what He has already left through the death of Christ in His "written will," and what He desires for us to have based on our relationship with Him. For us to possess all that we have coming to us, debt must be defeated. Refer to Appendix A and list beside each debt why it is a hostile enemy to the will of God (see Chapter 3 for ideas).

3. Understand Why Each Debt Arose
and Learn From Your Mistakes

There is a reason behind every action and circumstance. After listing your debts and understanding why they are enemies, it is then important to be honest with yourself as to why each debt arose. If you don't acknowledge the problem, Proverbs 26:11 will be your testimony.

Although it may be painful to admit to those causes, it will bring healing and eventual deliverance to your financial condition. Your motivation is in knowing that after God brings you out, you'll be able to help other people in their financial struggles. By admitting the causes, you identify your weaknesses, which will allow you to predict where the enemy will attack next.

The devil can tempt you only in an area of desire. James 1:14 says, "But every man is tempted, when he is drawn away of his own lust, and enticed." It is your own evil desires that lure you into sinning, even in the area of finances. An uncontrollable desire for new things is bait for sinful spending and is a normal cause of debt.

An evil desire is connected to a vital organ in your spirit, and poor spending habits give debt direct access to it, leaving it exposed. James 1:15 (AMP) says, "Then the evil desire, when it has conceived, gives birth to sin, and sin, when it is fully matured, brings forth death." The lust for new things will give birth to the sin of poor stewardship, and fully matured poor stewardship will cause death to your finances.

The key is knowing your weaknesses so you can abort your lust before it gives birth to sin. To do this, you must address the root, not just the symptoms. Even an exposed root can still bring forth fruit if it is not destroyed, so refer to Appendix A where all your debts are listed and beside each write why each bill arose. (See Chapter 6, "The Process.")

4. You Must See the Benefits of Being Debt-Free

In going back to our Scripture passage on being debt-free, David saw the benefits of destroying Goliath. They were so appealing that he made the soldiers repeat them because they seemed too good to be true. The benefits of being debt-free are motivation enough to tackle the largest of debts, but you must first see them. The three benefits listed in the passage were 1) the king will enrich him with great riches; 2) the king would give him his daughter as a wife; and 3) the king would make his house free in Israel (see 1 Sam. 17:25).

When you defeat debt, the same three benefits flow into your life. You have more money accessible to you, you can take care of your wife and family and provide more security, and you can help your family get out of debt. *In defeating debt, God (the king) sees that you can handle more money; therefore, He will trust you with more.* You have displayed that you understand money's purpose, power, and potential. The money that He is giving you now truly goes to you and not to debt.

When money is paid out to debt, the Kingdom is not furthered; therefore, God would rather let a sinner keep it until you can handle it than release it to you for you to waste. God hates things that are unnatural or go against their nature. Although most sinners naturally waste their money on sinful items, Christians should spend money on things that will help advance the Kingdom (see Prov. 10:16 TLB). God will release money to His people when we are in a position to multiply His resources for the Kingdom.

The king in First Samuel 17 was also willing to give this valiant, responsible man his daughter. Any person who could defeat such a fearsome enemy should be responsible and man enough to take care of a princess. God sees each of His daughters as princesses, but He is reluctant to release them to men who are irresponsible and plagued by debt. For God to release a wife (or husband) to you would cause you to contaminate her (him) and make her (him) vulnerable to the effects of your disease.

For men who are married, being debt-free allows you to provide your wife with a greater sense of security in knowing that all her needs will be provided for. Debt had previously enslaved her emotions and her will, but with its defeat, she is a new woman and it's easier for her to become all that God wants her to be in all areas (e.g., sexually). Then the honeymoon starts all over again.

Being debt-free also will cause your house or family to be free. When your bills are paid and debts are canceled, you can help other family members who are in debt get out through your wisdom, your testimony, and your money! Any curses of debt and poverty are now broken and there will be no more enslaved generations. Your family receives new hope, for if you did it, then they believe that they can do it. Close your eyes and imagine what life would be like if you were debt-free. Once you have this picture in your mind and the feeling in your spirit, never forget it. *Your imagination is designed to help you visit your future so that you will be motivated to leave your present. If you see what others don't see, you'll have what others don't have!* In Appendix A, list which goals can be accomplished once this debt is defeated.

5. Become Accountable to Someone Who Is Walking Victoriously and Who Has Your Best Interest in Mind

If you are in a poor financial condition, it is obvious that you will need help in getting your finances in order. *Pride keeps the financially crippled in a wheelchair.* Many times, people refuse to get help for their financial condition because of the shame that it would bring to their reputation. Being accountable oftentimes will give you the motivation to stick to your plan. People who have been where you are can tell you whether your goals are realistic, warn you of potential problems you may face, and provide possible solutions.

When Israel had no king, the Bible says that "every man did that which was right in his own eyes" (Judg. 21:25). A king speaks of accountability, order, and leadership. Because there was no one to help regulate the actions of the Israelites with guidance and accountability, they ran wild and got into various sins.

Your covenant partner should be someone with whom you can be totally transparent so he can assist you in identifying the root(s) of your financial problems. This person must be someone with whom you can share your credit report and every debt, bill, and source of income. Poor finances have the same nature as sin, meaning that if the devil can get you to hide your condition, it will slowly destroy you.

Secondly, you should be able to receive and adhere to your partner's biblical instruction. Proverbs 20:18 says, "Every purpose is established by counsel: and with good advice make war." This means that every intention you have is made firm by being accountable to someone. This person is there to motivate and encourage you, yet be firm and up front with you.

Thirdly, you must be willing to follow his example as an outline for victorious life. Psalm 37:37 says, "Mark the perfect man, and behold the upright: for the end of that man is peace." People need financial covering for the same reasons that they need spiritual covering. Notice in Scripture that *God never used anything that was uncovered*. Whether it was the Ark of the Covenant (see Ex. 25:11), the donkey for Jesus' triumphal entry (see Mk. 11:7), or even Jesus Himself (see Lk. 2:12), everything that was used by God was covered. And if God is going to use your finances, they have to be covered, whether by your spouse, a covenant partner, a pastor or an elder, or even a paid professional.

Your willingness to humble yourself to do these things is a sign that you really want deliverance, and God will honor it. What you paid for is what got you into financial problems. Would you be willing to pay someone to help you get out? On Appendix A, list the individuals to whom you will be accountable.

6. Destroy the Root of the Problem

The root can't just be exposed; it must also be *attacked* in order to be destroyed. For example, if a man was trying to get rid of his apples, merely picking all the fruit off the tree wouldn't solve the problem. It would just temporarily remove the apples. However, if he were to *cut* the tree's root, he would destroy the tree's *ability* to bring forth more apples. *The problem in finances is that people don't rob debt of its ability to bear fruit.* Simply paying the minimum monthly payment only picks the fruit off the tree. Paying the bill exposes the root; but understanding *why* you are in debt and eliminating the problem destroys its ability to bear more fruit.

One painful root that people must deal with is their friends. Many times, friends affect your spending habits and your attitude toward finances. Proverbs 29:3b says, "But he that keepeth company with harlots spendeth his substance." Harlots are loose in their lifestyles (e.g., designer clothes, excessive eating out, and a constant desire for new things). They spend without restraint, lack priorities, lack commitment to anything, are undisciplined, and don't see their personal value. Proverbs 13:20 says, "He that walketh with wise men shall be wise: but a companion of fools shall be destroyed." Your associations are vital to your development in every area of your life.

7. Make Cash Purchases Only; Don't Charge Anything

In Philippians 4:11-12, Paul discusses his ability to be content, regardless of his condition or circumstance. *Contentment is knowing how to control your spending when you can't control your income.* Many times people get into huge credit card debt because they aren't satisfied with the life that their cash income can give them. If cash had been paid, many luxury items would not have been bought. If you are serious about getting out of debt, don't use your credit card for anything, even if you commit to pay it off in 30 days.

Companies will offer you cash rebates for purchases, six months interest free, or a low introductory interest rate. But none of these amenities are worth the slavery of debt. If you lack the discipline to keep a card and not use it, close out all credit card accounts and remove your name from all credit card company mailing lists. (See Appendix B on how to do this.) Develop an emergency budget so that when problems arise, such as car trouble, hospital visits, or temporary unemployment, you won't be forced to use your credit card.

Remember that the cornerstone of the devil's attack is deception, and that debt and the devil are twins. Therefore, debt will try to deceive you into thinking that you can pay off the balance in 30 days. If you previously had trouble paying the balance in 30 days, what makes you think that this time will be different? Keep in mind that every new debt you incur is more responsibility, and the important thing in becoming debt-free is to have no financial obligations except for life's necessities. *Remember, financial healing can begin only after the plastic surgery*, so cut up those credit cards now!

8. Control Your Spending and Follow Your Budget

A budget is like the out-of-bounds lines in football. They provide boundaries for the teams to operate in. Whenever the offensive team goes out of bounds, their scoring drive is momentarily stopped. Your scoring drive is the elimination of debt, and whenever you exceed your budget, your drive is stopped. Now you must "huddle" or regroup your offensive attack.

The defensive strategy of debt is money leaks. Debt creates money leaks, then comes with deception and gets you to use your credit card when an unexpected expense arises. That's why there should be an emergency budget implemented to handle the unexpected. *Every bill that's unprepared for will be unexpected.* You prepare by setting money aside for potential problems (see Prov. 22:3), or by having a proven plan to reduce expenses.

By paying your bills on time, you give yourself a sense of accomplishment, which provides the motivation to attack debt. Use this motivation to offset the depression that debt releases. Before you can *destroy* debt you must *control* spending. Nothing can be destroyed until it is first controlled. If spending is not controlled, the extra money that was to be used to attack debt is used instead to stay current—and another defeat adds more depression.

In Matthew 12:29, Jesus says that before a strong man can be overcome, he must first be bound. In other words, before his house can be destroyed, he must first be controlled. The strong-man of spending must first be controlled before the stronghold of *debt* can be defeated. Focus on one battle at a time. If you don't, you will become frustrated, your efforts will be divided, and you will stand no chance of victory (see Mt. 12:25; Jas. 1:8).

9. Identify Your Weapons

Many ask, "Where will I get money to fight debt?" The answer is found in Second Kings 4:2, when Elisha said to the widow, "What hast thou in the house?" Everything that you need to defeat debt is in your possession—you just have to identify it. *The only people who go to war without weapons are those who either don't intend to fight or don't intend to win.* **God wants to take what you have to create what you need.** All you have to do is give it to Him.

In Appendix C we have listed some weapons that people have, including bills. After identifying what weapons you have, you must determine how you will make each of these weapons work for you and "schedule when they will be available for duty." By doing this you can construct a strategic plan of attack.

10. Lay Out the Plan Bill By Bill

The Bible tells us in Habakkuk 2:2 to "...*Write* the vision, and *make it plain upon tables*, that he may *run that readeth* it." This is because an *unwritten* plan is impossible to follow. There is a power in writing things down that gives focus, motivation, and hope. Laying out each bill allows you to thoroughly investigate and study your enemy. A written plan will allow you and your spouse to be in agreement, track your progress, and eliminate frustration. You will know exactly when you are scheduled to get out of debt. Bills will leave a tracking record from your spending pattern that can trace where the enemy (debt) was able to infiltrate.

No sports team goes into a game without first watching some film of their opponent. By doing this, they learn strengths, weaknesses, and tendencies of the opposing team. This makes *organization* of their attack more efficient. If you don't organize your finances, you'll *agonize* over them. In First Samuel 17:34-37, David testifies of his victory over the lion and the bear. This gave him the *confidence* that the same God who gave him victory over the lion and the bear would give him victory over Goliath.

We generally recommend that people attack the smallest bill first and, once it's paid off, keep it as a testimony and motivation builder. (Remember, Israel kept the 12 smooth stones after they crossed the Jordan [see Josh. 4].) In deciding which bill to attack first, you must consider interest rates, tax deductibility, and the amount of money that each will free up. Some couples are more motivated psychologically by having a bill paid off than by having the extra money. Each couple must consider what motivates them the most.

As you work your way up to Goliath (the largest bill), keep in mind that it was God who helped you defeat even the smallest bill and that He's big enough to grace you to defeat the Goliath in your finances. Never pay extra on multiple bills. You won't see as much progress and are likely to become frustrated. Concentrate on one bill and use any extra money to attack it until it is defeated.

After David defeated Goliath, he decapitated him and took his sword (see 1 Sam. 17:49-51). When you defeat debt, you cut the head off the monster of poverty and acquire a new weapon to attack debt (the weapon/money that was used to attack the last debt, now used to attack the next debt) and so gain dominion over your finances. Never throw away paid off bills; keep them as testimonies and reminders in the event that you consider going back into debt.

Reward yourself after a bill is paid off to keep your motivation and to get out of the slave mentality. Most bills, with the exception of your mortgage, can be paid off in two years or less. *Imagine two years of sacrifice in exchange for a lifetime in*

Canaan land. In Hebrews 12:2, the Bible says that Jesus was able to endure the cross because of the joy that was set before Him. You must see the benefits of becoming debt-free if you're going to have the motivation to strive for it. In summation, the six critical points of laying out your plan are as follows:

1. Put your plan in writing and have it reviewed by your covenant partner.
2. Attack the smallest bill first, or whichever one motivates you the most.
3. Attack one debt at a time.
4. Identify and use all your weapons to attack debt.
5. After a debt is paid off, use the majority of the money to attack the next debt as well as reward yourself and help someone else get out of debt.
6. Keep your paid off debts as a memorial like Israel did with the 12 stones.

11. Attack and Be Relentless

It is important to remember that with every debt you defeat, your army (wealth) should get larger. Debt's defeat reminds us of what Jesus did to the devil (see Col. 2:14-15). To attack is to come against with the intent to *pay off* and not just *pay on.* If you aren't relentless in your attack, debt will rise up against you and eventually overtake you.

When the lion and the bear came and stole the lamb, David "went out after him, and smote him" (1 Sam. 17:35). David's original intention was just to get back what the enemy took from him. He didn't kill the enemy until it rose up against him. If it were possible to obtain from debt what it has taken without destroying it, that might be an option. But because it's not, we have no choice but to destroy debt and any trace of its existence.

You must be the aggressor in order to overtake debt. Never let up on it until you are certain that it is defeated. Don't fall short in your slaughter of debt; totally destroy the problem! In Judges 1, the Israelites had instructions to totally destroy the Canaanites because God knew that if the Israelites let them linger, they would influence His people to eventually turn from Him. But the Bible says that "when Israel was strong, that they put the Canaanites to tribute, and did not utterly drive them out" (Judg. 1:28).

Many times Christians get slack in attacking the enemy when they experience some progress. The Israelites let the Canaanites linger because they believed that they could handle the situation, and eventually they fell into all types of sin and idolatry. The same thing happens today when we believe that we have something under control. We become passive and allow debts and bills to linger until eventually their influence swells and debt overtakes us again.

Debt is not something to play with. It is a powerful force that the enemy uses to destroy your seed, your will, and your destiny. That's why we wrote this book. We have paid tuition in the class of debt and are sharing with others what we've learned. It costs more than it's worth. Therefore, if we can save you some money in your financial education, we will.

12. Help Someone Else Get Out of Debt

Whenever you sow into someone else's life, it creates a harvest in yours. The seed that you sow will determine the fruit that you reap. If you sow a seed that helps someone get out of debt, then your harvest will be something that can help you get out of debt. In reaping a harvest, there are four necessary elements: the sowing of the seed, the ground, the cultivation, and the watering (see Mk. 4:3-9).

When you help others, you water the seed you sowed (see Prov. 11:24-25). There can be no harvest unless a seed gets water. Leviticus 25:47-55 describes how, in the Year of Jubilee, a kinsman redeemer would buy servants out of bondage. God blessed Abraham to be a blessing (see Gen. 12:2). If God is going to help you get out of debt, then you must be willing to help someone else out. By doing this you reveal the invisible nature of God.

Man is the highest form of creation; therefore, he is the highest form of expression of God. Family members who are sinners are able to see the attributes of God despite their sinful condition when there is someone who is willing to reveal Him in a tangible way.

In Acts 2:43-47, the believers had "all things common" and were able to help one another because they were not plagued by bills. Additionally, this expression of love, commitment, and financial freedom gave them favor with all the people, and God added to the Church daily (see Acts 2:47). Giving your money to help others in debt shows that your faith is in God to deliver you and not in money. Remember that what you make happen for others, God will make happen for you.

Chapter 9

The Possibilities of Debt

Throughout this book we have exposed the true nature of debt as an enemy to the revealed will of God for your life. However, even debt has possibilities. We are still against the *concepts* and *abuse* of debt; but Romans 8:28 says that "...*all* things work together for good to them that love God, to them who are the called according to His purpose." Therefore, there must be some good that can come from debt. It's found in First Samuel 17:8-9.

In this passage Goliath challenges the Israelites, commanding them to release a warrior to fight with him. The terms were that, if Goliath won, Israel would serve the Philistines; but if the Israelites won, then the Philistines would serve Israel. In various places in this book we have referred to our "David and Goliath Theory." If you are David and your debt is Goliath, then whatever debt you defeat should "serve you," or become an investment.

Debt should never keep you totally subservient; you should overtake your debt and allow it to work for you. In this chapter, we will discuss ways to make debt work more in your favor. *Do not use this chapter as a basis or excuse to get into debt.* Continue to keep the attitude and advice that we have been giving throughout the book. This is a chapter that will simply give you strategies to turn what the devil meant for evil into good until you can defeat it.

1. Only Borrow When the Return Will Be Greater

Borrowing should be like investing, where you always get out more than you put in. In Second Kings 4:1-7, the woman borrowed jars to get oil, but her return was far greater—she was able to pay back her debtors and have money left over. God allowed Israel to participate in "time borrowing" of the Egyptians' jewels of silver and gold, such as they would need to get them out of Egypt and into the Promised Land (see Ex. 3:19-22; 11:2). Borrowing was permitted for a short period of time in order to meet needs to fulfill God's purpose. *God's initial purpose for debt was to help those in need, without charging interest* (see Ex. 22:25; Lev. 25:35-36).

Borrowing is never divine if it is for an unreasonable period of time, is based on the loan, and does not yield a greater return. If you borrow money to purchase items, the items should appreciate in value and/or increase your value, thus providing you with benefits even after the debt is paid off (see Appendix D). Things that you should *never* borrow for include food, clothes, trips, or personal items that are non-necessities such as nail polish, jewelry, accessories, etc. Even hygiene products should be paid for with cash. Things that provide a greater return include homes, education, starting a business, or purchasing rental property.

2. Debt Disciplines You for Saving and Investing

If you can be disciplined enough to pay bills, then you can be disciplined enough to pay yourself. *Savings is the one bill that almost everyone is delinquent in paying.* The same tactics that were used to pay your debts every month can be used to save money every month. If you had bills automatically drafted from your checking account, have that same amount automatically drafted into your savings account once bills are paid off. The bills have trained you to set aside money monthly, regardless of what comes up. The discipline that's developed is far more important than the money saved because it will spill over into every area of your life.

Debt has now switched roles from master to servant (see the beginning of this chapter). The debt, which brought great depression and sorrow, is now a great source of excitement and joy. You are guaranteed at least an 18 percent return on your investment—the 18 percent you were paying on your credit card—plus the interest you receive on your savings and investments.

When you consistently save, you allow your money to work as hard for you as you work for it. There is an enhancement of your financial portfolio and it shows lenders that you are consistent. The money that is saved greatly reduces the need to borrow in the future. When debt is not turned into an investment, you risk making your accomplishments null and void.

You will never be satisfied by debt. Coming out just to go right back in is foolishness. God wants you to have nice things, but there is a time and a season for everything. Egypt represents being in debt; the Promised Land represents living in abundance; but first they had to go through the wilderness, which is a time of trusting God and represents saving, investing, and budgeting. You're free but you haven't inherited the promise. Remember, your season of saving precedes your season of spending.

3. Use Your Debt to Establish a *Good* Name

When finance companies look to determine whether or not you're a good risk, they never consider your contribution statement from the church, your year-end pledge, or the number of auxiliaries you're in. Your credit report is their means of determination. *A credit report is written verification of your integrity.* It directly impacts interest rates, employment opportunities, cost of insurance, housing (renting of an apartment), and your ability to obtain a loan.

Christians will many times try to use Jesus' name to do what their name is no good to do. Jesus said that in His name we would cast out devils, speak with new tongues, etc. (see Mk. 16:17). He did *not* say that we would spend foolishly, charge unnecessary items, or get into unnecessary debt. Because our credit report is in *our* name and is strengthened or weakened by *our* name, then we are responsible for its condition. It is in our name that we purchase cars, homes, land, and things for our spouse and family. It is in Jesus' name that we ask for deliverance in healing. It is imperative that we know which name to use.

When your good name is established, it enhances your witness, influence, and self-esteem. If you presently have poor credit, your debt can become a way to build your good name. The best way to establish or reestablish your name is simply to pay your debts on time. This will build a strong credit profile that will allow you to borrow money cheaper in the future.

Here is the strategy on how to use debt to rebuild your credit. We recommend this only because the return is greater than the debt. Obtain a secured loan from the bank by asking for a loan; then use *their* money to purchase a CD that is given back to them as the collateral. The banks have their money in a no-risk loan. The benefit is that you've enhanced your credit rating. (Bank loans are the best possible reference.) When the loan is paid in full, you have an investment, you've developed discipline, you've built a relationship with a banker who knows and trusts you, and your confidence and self-esteem are built.

This process can be repeated to build a stronger credit profile and to enhance your savings. This new, stronger reference also helps to reduce the effects of "weak" credit references such as finance and rent-to-own companies. The long-term monetary cost of borrowing to rebuild your credit is in your favor. In the future, when you borrow at a lower rate on *each* $10,000, a 4 percent rate decline saves you $19 per month for life. Consider Proverbs 22:1, where Solomon says, "A good name is rather to be chosen than great riches, and loving favour rather than silver and gold." We must have a good name in order to exercise full authority in the earth and occupy until He comes.

4. Borrow From Yourself

God has declared that He wants us to be self-sufficient (see 2 Cor. 9:8 AMP) and to lend and not borrow (see Deut. 15:6). Therefore, it is possible that we could lend to ourselves instead of borrowing from others, for when we borrow from others we become slaves to them (see Prov. 22:7). Following are six options for you to borrow from yourself.

Option #1: Many employers offer a 401k plan to their employees. This is one of the best sources to borrow from. The rates are lower on the loan, saving you money; and the interest that you pay is paid back to you. This money is no longer invested in the market, but *you* become the investment. After the loan is paid, continue to have the same amount of money drafted out of your paycheck, using debt to develop discipline to save. Remember, *if you leave your job, you must pay the loan back to yourself within a specified time or it is considered a premature withdrawal. Then you will be taxed and the 10 percent early withdrawal penalty applies.*

Option #2: Another method for people with whole life insurance is to borrow from the cash surrender value of the policy. This is money that has accumulated from the overpayment of your premium. This money has a low interest rate; however, it does reduce your death benefit. The recommended strategy for most people would be to secure a term policy with a reputable company, which would have a much lower monthly payment. (Utilize an insurance quote service to help you find the best policy.) Obtain your cash surrender value (use it to attack debt), then cancel your whole life policy. Understand that *your* cash surrender value from overpayment of your premium would go to the insurance company and not to you in the event of death.

Option #3: If you are a person who has some extra cash saved, you could borrow from yourself and pay it back within a certain amount of time with interest. Though this takes a lot of discipline, the rewards can be great.

Option #4: You could also use your money as collateral for a loan, negotiating a better interest rate and having the payment drafted out of your account. Though you've created a debt, the interest rate should be between 2 and 4 percent lower than normal because the bank has collateral and the likelihood of you defaulting is minimal.

Option #5: This strategy works especially well with those who break even with taxes. You could acquire a six-month, interest-free loan from the IRS to pay off debt and bills. The first six months of the year, adjust your withholdings where there are no taxes taken out. (Consult your tax preparer for specific instructions.) Use the extra money to get out of debt and save. Then, the final six months of the year, have double the normal amount of taxes taken out. This will cause you to break even for the year. Though you have less income for the final six months, you also have less bills; therefore, the impact of your reduced check is neutralized. This will not alarm the IRS. They will consider your taxes paid evenly throughout the year.

Option #6: You could borrow from your own tax refund by changing your allowances as previously mentioned (Form W-4), and adjust your Earned Income Credit (Form W-5) to get it in your paycheck. A tax refund means that you have had too much tax withheld and are giving the IRS or your state an interest-free loan. There are various ways that you can borrow from yourself; the key is identifying all your assets so you can know your possibilities.

5. Tax Benefits

We stated earlier in the book that you should *never borrow for tax deductions.* However, there may be times in life when you must borrow. Therefore, listed below are strategies to get the best tax benefit when you *must* borrow.

1. If you know that you will have to spend money in January (e.g., church pledge, child care, property taxes, and mortgage payment), put it on your credit card in December. This allows you to deduct it on your current year's tax return. (You've accelerated your tax deduction by 12 months.) You receive a tax benefit this year versus waiting a full year. This is an excellent strategy to use in a year where you've moved up to a higher tax bracket because of something unusual (e.g., 401k distribution). *Make sure that you pay the credit card off in January!*

2. Most interest is not tax deductible, but some still is. If you must pay interest, at least make it tax deductible. The two most common forms of deductible interest (non-business) are mortgage (or home equity) and charity. You can convert your non-deductible interest, such as for credit cards, car loans, and loans from finance companies, into a home equity/mortgage. It's deductible and the rates are much lower, creating a double savings. *Remember, debt consolidation without problem elimination creates financial frustration.*

3. If you *must* carry a balance on your credit card (*we do not advise this!*), make it gifts to charity (tithes, offerings, and pledges) versus clothes, shoes, and other non-necessities. Use the money that you give in church to buy things with and use the card that you buy things with to give your tithe and offerings. *Do not make this a habit! This is a tax strategy to get a greater deduction on specific occasions, not a recommended method of giving!* The interest will be tax deductible.

6. Negotiate a Pay Off With Vendors

The only way that you can get out of paying your debt without violating Psalm 37:21 is for the *creditor* to release you. The only way that a word from God can release you from your debt is if He also miraculously provides the money. Outside of that you *must* pay your creditors.

If you have old debts that you have not paid on (don't go out and create debt), you can negotiate a pay off with vendors. Many will accept 50 cents for every dollar that you owe. Therefore, borrowing to pay off a negotiated debt can be beneficial if you pay off the loan in a short time and the interest rates and amount borrowed are not extremely high. (Appendix E in the back of the book provides a good illustration of this point.) Get your vendor to enhance your credit rating; they have the authority to do this. Also, make sure that it is shown as a *pay off* and not a *charge off*. (A pay off implies payment in full; a charge off means they had to write it off.)

Be sure to consider all your circumstances and get all agreements in writing. Before you negotiate with a vendor, you must know exactly where the money is coming from. The amount of money that the vendors release you from paying does become taxable income.

7. Make Debt an Investment

The best way to defeat an enemy is to make it do what is contrary to its nature and battle plan. Remember the Scripture in First Samuel 17:8-10 where Goliath spoke of the terms of battle. With every debt you defeat, your army should get larger because your debts have now become investments. If the debt that is paid off has an interest rate of 18 percent, that's a guaranteed 18 percent return on your investment. The same amount of money that was going to pay off your debt is now going into an investment for you—that which had you enslaved now serves you.

If there are additional debts, split up this amount between paying off other debts (debt elimination) and investing in your future (wealth accumulation). Debt is a serious and dangerous enemy that must be handled seriously to be defeated. With proper planning, conviction, determination, and most of all prayer and meditation on the Word of God, debt can and will be defeated in your life!

Appendixes

Appendix A — Debt Reduction Schedule

Debt	Why it's an enemy	Why it arose	Goals after debt is paid	Mo. pmt.	Jan.	Feb.	Mar.	April	May	June	July	Aug.	Sept.	Oct.	Nov.	Dec.

Individuals whom I will be accountable to:

_____

_____

Note: You may photocopy this schedule and/or enlarge it for your convenience.

Appendix B

Removing Your Name From Mailing Lists

Listed below are the three major credit bureaus. These companies sell their mailing lists to various companies for pre-approved credit cards. To have your name removed, you will need to call each one of them and carefully follow their instructions.

Equifax:	1-800-556-4711
Transunion:	1-800-680-7293
Experian:	1-800-353-0809

To have your name purged from many direct-mail company files, write to the following address and give your name and address:

Direct Marketing Association's Mail Preference Service
P.O. Box 9008
Farmingdale, NY 11735

Additional companies get your name from credit bureaus. You can call 1-888-567-8688 to request that the major bureaus not share or exchange your name.

Appendix C — Weapons for Warfare

Weapon to Use	Action Plan	Date Money Available	One Time Amount	Monthly Amount
Increase my tax allowance	Find out from my accountant how many allowances I can claim w/o owing IRS; obtain W-4 from payroll dept. or IRS; change allowance; submit to payroll dept.	6/1		$75
Reduce my expenses using the Ten/Ten theory	List all the ways I spend money; under each, list ways to reduce expenses; get cost cutting ideas from friends and family members.	5/15 - List spending ways 5/22 - Collect ideas 6/1 - Implement		$100
Get my earned income credit in advance	Complete Form W-5 and give to employer, thus reducing my tax refund but increasing my check (new one must be done every year).	Obtain W-5 - 4/1 Earned Income Credit - 5/1		$50
Obtain cash surrender value	With my whole life insurance policy, get the cash buildup from excess premium payments; pay off bills. (This will reduce the death benefit.)	6/1	$500	
Get a part-time job	Consider the following: Will the hours conflict with family and God; how long will I work the job; how will I use the money; is it something I enjoy doing?	7/1		$200
Develop tax strategies	For every $1 deduction, I save 15 cents in taxes; talk with accountant on strategies.	8/1 - Get strategies 12/1 - Implement	$400	
Start a business	Identify a hobby; turn talents into a business with low start-up cost.	6/15		$75
Sell unused assets	Have family fund-raisers such as yard sales or rummage sales.	8/1	$300	
Get an IRS six-month, interest-free loan	For the first six months of the year have no taxes withheld; last six months have double taxes withheld; pay off debt and be prepared for last six months when withholdings are doubled.	Start at the beginning of the upcoming year, or possibly start 7/1 and go for three months instead of six		$150
Work overtime	Request overtime; use it exclusively for debt (identify the exact debt to attack); reward myself with 1/2 of overtime when bill is paid off.	7/15		$50
Collect old debt from friends	Show them how to create extra income.	7/28	$300	
Totals			$1,500	$700

Activating Your Weapon

(Dates money will be available per Appendix C)

Weapons to use	April	May	June	July	Aug.	Sept.	Oct.	Nov.	Dec.
Increase my tax allowance	0	0	75	75	75	75	75	75	75
Reduce my expenses using the Ten/Ten theory	0	0	100	100	100	100	100	100	100
Get my earned income credit in advance	0	50	50	50	50	50	50	50	50
Obtain cash surrender value	0	0	500	0	0	0	0	0	0
Get a part-time job	0	0	0	200	200	200	200	200	200
Develop tax strategies	0	0	0	0	0	0	0	0	400
Start a business	0	0	75	75	75	75	75	75	75
Sell unused assets	0	0	0	0	300	0	0	0	0
Get an IRS six-month, interest free loan	0	0	0	150	150	150	0	0	0
Work overtime	0	0	0	50	50	50	50	50	50
Collect old debt from friends	0	0	0	300	0	0	0	0	0
TOTALS	0	50	800	1000	1000	700	550	550	950

Based on Appendix C, this schedule outlines by month how much extra money you will have to attack debt and the source. The plan is to attact the smallest debt first (some exceptions apply) and to continue to pay the regular amount on each debt. For the debt you are attacking, you would pay the regular payment, plus the extra available money outlined in this schedule, plus the regular payment from any paid-off debt or debts. Repeat this process until each debt is defeated. To activate Proverbs 11:24-25, you may want to tithe off the paid-off debt or help someone else get out of debt.

Appendix D

To Borrow or Not to Borrow?

Only borrow when the return will be greater. Outlined below is a comparison of things we recommend to borrow for, versus things that you should not borrow for.

When the return is greater:
1. Buying a car for work.
2. Borrowing to rebuild credit.
3. Buying a house.
4. Purchasing rental property.
5. Starting or expanding a business.
6. Furthering your education.
7. Giving to your church.
8. Negotiating to pay off a debt.

When the return is *not* greater:
1. Buying clothes.
2. Purchasing food.
3. Obtaining furniture (there are some exceptions).
4. Taking trips.
5. Purchasing jewelry (there are some exceptions).
6. Buying personal items.
7. Shopping for holiday and/or back-to-school purchases.
8. Giving loans to friends.

Appendix E

Example of Borrowing for a Negotiated Pay Off

Past due debt:	$2000.00
Negotiated pay off amount:	$1000.00
Savings:	$1000.00
Borrow:	$1000.00 at 12 percent for one year
Payment:	$ 88.85
Interest payment:	$ 66.20
Net savings:	**$ 933.80**

Note: Don't forget to identify your weapons as outlined in Chapter 8 and attack this debt. Additionally, once the loan is paid off, continue to pay yourself or attack debt.

For additional information, bookings for workshops (at which this book is offered), a personal financial consultation, or assistance with bringing your ministry into compliance with IRS and state regulations, contact:

William V. Thompson & Associates, Inc.
1600 East Wendover Avenue, Suite I
Greensboro, NC 27405
Phone: (336) 272-2363
Fax: (336) 272-2967
E-mail: wvthompson@williamvthompson.com

D *Destiny Image*
New Releases

8:16

Other

Destiny Image titles
you will enjoy reading

FATHER, FORGIVE US!

by Jim W. Goll.

What is holding back a worldwide "great awakening"? What hinders the Church all over the world from rising up and bringing in the greatest harvest ever known? The answer is simple: sin! God is calling Christians today to take up the mantle of identificational intercession and repent for the sins of the present and past; for the sins of our fathers; for the sins of the nations. Will you heed the call? This book shows you how!

ISBN 0-7684-2025-3

MANHOOD GOD'S STYLE

by Rev. Wilbur Conway.

Society is hurting for true men—God's style of men—who, with Jesus as their example, are willing to accept responsibility and serve faithfully in their families, churches, and communities as priest, provider, and protector. These are men of integrity, holiness, wisdom, prayer, the Word, and the Spirit. Here Wilbur Conway challenges men of God to rise up and set the standard for true manhood—God's style!

ISBN 1-56043-318-3

THE THRESHOLD OF GLORY

Compiled by Dotty Schmitt.

What does it mean to experience the "glory of God"? How does it come? These women of God have crossed that threshold, and it changed not only their ministries but also their very lives! Here Dotty Schmitt and Sue Ahn, Bonnie Chavda, Pat Chen, Dr. Flo Ellers, Brenda Kilpatrick, and Varle Rollins teach about God's glorious presence and share how it transformed their lives.

ISBN 0-7684-2044-X

ONLY BELIEVE

by Don Stewart.

Who was A.A. Allen, John Dowie, Maria Woodworth-Etter, and William Branham? Who were these and the many other people who picked up the mantle of the healing evangelist in the twentieth century? What was their legacy? Don Stewart, who was mentored by A.A. Allen and had contact with most of his contemporaries in this widespread movement, gives an inside look into their lives and ministries. This incredible, firsthand witness account of the events and people who have shaped our current Christian heritage will astound you with how God takes frail, human vessels, pours out His anointing, and enables them to do mighty exploits for Him!

ISBN 1-56043-340-X

Available at your local Christian bookstore.

Internet: http://www.reapernet.com

Other
Destiny Image titles
you will enjoy reading

THE MARTYRS' TORCH
by Bruce Porter.

In every age of history, darkness has threatened to extinguish the light. But also in every age of history, heroes and heroines of the faith rose up to hold high the torch of their testimony—witnesses to the truth of the gospel of Jesus Christ. On a fateful spring day at Columbine High, others lifted up their torches and joined the crimson path of the martyrs' way. We cannot forget their sacrifice. A call is sounding forth from Heaven: "Who will take up the martyrs' torch which fell from these faithful hands?" Will you?
ISBN 0-7684-2046-6

THE LOST PASSIONS OF JESUS
by Donald L. Milam, Jr.
What motivated Jesus to pursue the cross? What inner strength kept His feet on the path laid before Him? Time and tradition have muted the Church's knowledge of the passions that burned in Jesus' heart, but if we want to—if we dare to—we can still seek those same passions. Learn from a close look at Jesus' own life and words and from the writings of other dedicated followers the passions that enflamed the Son of God and changed the world forever!
ISBN 0-9677402-0-7

POWER, HOLINESS, AND EVANGELISM
Contributing Authors: *Gordon Fee, Steve Beard, Dr. Michael Brown, Pablo Bottari, Pablo Deiros, Chris Heuertz, Scott McDermott, Carlos Mraida, Mark Nysewander, Stephen Seamands, Harvey Brown Jr.*
Compiled by *Randy Clark*
Many churches today stress holiness but lack power, while others display great power but are deficient in personal holiness and Christian character. If we really want to win our world for Christ, we must bring both holiness and power back into our lives. A church on fire will draw countless thousands to her light.
ISBN 1-56043-345-0

THE RADICAL CHURCH
by Bryn Jones.
The world of the apostles and the world of today may look a lot different, but there is one thing that has not changed: the need for a radical Church in a degenerate society. We still need a church, a body of people, who will bring a hard-hitting, totally unfamiliar message: Jesus has come to set us free! Bryn Jones of Ansty, Coventry, United Kingdom, an apostolic leader to numerous churches across the world, will challenge your view of what church is and what it is not. Be prepared to learn afresh of the Church that Jesus Christ is building today!
ISBN 0-7684-2022-9

Available at your local Christian bookstore.

Internet: http://www.reapernet.com

Other
Destiny Image titles
you will enjoy reading

AN INVITATION TO FRIENDSHIP:
From the Father's Heart, Volume 2
by Charles Slagle.
Our God is a Father whose heart longs for His children to sit and talk with Him in fellowship and oneness. This second volume of intimate letters from the Father to you, His child, reveals His passion, dreams, and love for you. As you read them, you will find yourself drawn ever closer within the circle of His embrace. The touch of His presence will change your life forever!
ISBN 0-7684-2013-X

HIDDEN TREASURES OF THE HEART
by Donald Downing.
What is hidden in your heart? Your heart is the key to life—both natural and spiritual. If you aren't careful with your heart, you run the risk of becoming vulnerable to the attacks of the enemy. This book explains the changes you need to make to ensure that your commitment to God is from the heart and encourages you to make those changes. Don't miss out on the greatest blessing of all—a clean heart!
ISBN 1-56043-315-9

THE ASCENDED LIFE
by Bernita J. Conway.
A believer does not need to wait until Heaven to experience an intimate relationship with the Lord. When you are born again, your life becomes His, and He pours His life into yours. Here Bernita Conway explains from personal study and experience the truth of "abiding in the Vine," the Lord Jesus Christ. When you grasp this understanding and begin to walk in it, it will change your whole life and relationship with your heavenly Father!
ISBN 1-56043-337-X

DREAMS IN THE SPIRIT, VOL. 1
by Bart Druckenmiller.
We all want to hear the word of the Lord. Nevertheless, many people don't. They limit how God speaks, not recognizing His voice throughout life's experiences, including dreams in the night and "daydreams" born of the Spirit. As a result, our lives lack vision and destiny. This book will introduce you to how God speaks through dreams and visions. It will give you hope that you, too, can learn to hear God's voice in your dreams and fulfill all that He speaks to you.
ISBN 1-56043-346-9

Available at your local Christian bookstore.

Internet: http://www.reapernet.com